Routledge Revivals

Political Change in Spain

First published in 1989, *Political Change in Spain* provides a stimulating and innovative account of Spain's maturing democracy since 1982. Challenging the accepted wisdom that Spanish democracy is a fragile plant, the author demonstrates its strong roots and healthy growth in the context of the European Community. He argues that, despite the problems of economic transformation, Spain's political attachments to Western Europe suggest that the Spanish economy will benefit in the long run from its increasing integration with its neighbours. The book also analyses the continuing threat to stability posed by separatist aspirations in the Basque country, in the context of the experiments with autonomous regional governments. This book will be valuable to anyone looking for a succinct introduction to changes in Spain, as well as to students of Western European politics, women's studies and the Spanish language.

Political Change in Spain

Edward Moxon-Browne

Routledge
Taylor & Francis Group

First published in 1989
By Routledge

This edition first published in 2024 by Routledge
4 Park Square, Milton Park, Abingdon, Oxon, OX14 4RN
and by Routledge
605 Third Avenue, New York, NY 10017

Routledge is an imprint of the Taylor & Francis Group, an informa business

Publisher's Note
The publisher has gone to great lengths to ensure the quality of this reprint but points out that some imperfections in the original copies may be apparent.

Disclaimer
The publisher has made every effort to trace copyright holders and welcomes correspondence from those they have been unable to contact.

ISBN: 978-1-032-73633-4 (hbk)
ISBN: 978-1-003-46522-5 (ebk)
ISBN: 978-1-032-73638-9 (pbk)

Book DOI 10.4324/9781003465225

Political Change in Spain

Edward Moxon-Browne

ROUTLEDGE
London and New York

First published 1989
by Routledge
11 New Fetter Lane, London EC4 4EE
29 West 35th Street, New York, NY 10001

Typeset directly from the publisher's word processor disks by
NWL Editorial Services, Langport, Somerset

Printed and bound in Great Britain by
MacKays of Chatham PLC, Chatham, Kent

British Library Cataloguing in Publication Data

Moxon-Browne, Edward
    Political change in Spain.
        1. Spain, Political development, history
        I. Title
        320.946
        ISBN 0-415-02322-X

Library of Congress Cataloging-in-Publication Data

Moxon-Browne, Edward.
    Political change in Spain / Edward Moxon-Browne
        p.   cm.
        ISBN 0-415-02322-X
    1. Spain–Politics and government–1975- 2. Representative
government and representation–Spain–History–20th century.
3. Regionalism–Spain–History–20th century. 4. Women in
politics–Spain–History–20th century. 5. Spain–Relations–
Europe. 6. Europe–Relations–Spain. I. Title.
DP272.M69   1989
320.946–dc20   89-10421
                                                       CIP

Contents

Preface

Spain's rapid and peaceful transition from dictatorship to democracy has understandably attracted a considerable amount of attention (Maravall 1982; Carr and Fusi 1979; Lopez-Pintor 1982; Gunther *et al.* 1986). Less well charted are political developments since 1982, and it is this period of consolidation that forms the focus of this book. Although the shape of the Spanish political system is not yet clearly defined, the contours are becoming visible. It is possible now to discern the implications of democratic politics for the Spanish people, and draw conclusions from Spain's firm attachment to Western Europe. It is, perhaps, due to Spain's membership of the European Economic Community, above all, that a knowledge of Spain's internal political dynamics becomes a necessity and not a luxury for all West Europeans. In the common enterprise, in which all members of the European Economic Community are engaged, the process of harmonization and the achievement of common policies, place a high premium on mutual awareness.

This book makes the basic assumption that political change can best be viewed simultaneously from a variety of angles. In their discussion of distinct but related themes, the five chapters of this book seek to present a cumulative picture of political change in Spain since 1982. Earlier books on Spain agonized over the fragility of the country's nascent democracy: in Chapter 1 we argue not only that democracy itself has become secure, but that earlier fears of its demise may have been misplaced. In Chapter 2, we suggest that while the Spanish party system may appear similar to other West European party systems, the identification of policies with personalities poses a special threat to a party's cohesion and its responsiveness to public opinion. If there is a threat to the democratic system in Spain, it may stem from the federalist aspirations of the regions. In Chapter 3, we analyse the competitive tensions between the centre and the periphery, tensions that may only be exacerbated by international economic forces. One of the clearest indications of political change has been in relation to women: in Chapter 4, the absorption of feminist demands into the political system is portrayed as both a success and a drawback for the women's movement. The external environment intrudes as never before into Spanish politics and, in Chapter 5, it is suggested that membership of NATO and the EEC will leave indelible marks on domestic politics while, at the same time, force the resolution of several ambiguities in Spanish foreign policy.

Throughout the discussion of these themes, an attempt has been made to relate Spanish events to the broader West European scene; and to set developments in Spanish politics in a wider theoretical context. It is hoped that this will enable the reader to judge the nature of political change in Spain against the background of change elsewhere, whilst retaining some sense of what is unique in the Spanish experience.

Acknowledgements

I would like to thank the Librarian at the European University Institute in Florence for allowing me to work there in August 1986. I owe a special debt to Patricia-Anne who tolerated my long hours in front of the word processor. This book is dedicated to her. As always, I owe an unfathomable debt to my parents.

Chapter one
Democracy: the seeds of change

Introduction

In this first chapter we consider some of the factors that are likely to be relevant to our theme of political change: the geography of Spain; its population; its recent history; the social structure; the contours of economic development; and rapidly changing mores that are reflected in literature, in the media and, most importantly, in the minds of the Spanish people.

Although political change can be regarded as a universal phenomenon, there is infinite variety in the forms that it takes and the speeds at which it unfolds. Political change may be gradual or it may be abrupt; it may be imperceptible or cataclysmic. Its character may be influenced by a whole host of factors such as economic development, geography, technological progress, social structure, prevailing ideologies, and the qualities of political leaders.

Political change manifests itself most dramatically in those revolutions and wars that usher in new epochs in the political life of a country: the French Revolution of 1789 or the Russian Revolution of 1917 immediately spring to mind. But political change also takes place within the most stable political systems. Stability should not be confused with absence of change: it is only that the changes are evolutionary rather than revolutionary. Nor should political change necessarily be associated with 'progress'. In retrospect, we may choose to regard a political change as 'progressive' but it all depends on where we stand. The USSR undoubtedly welcomed the advent of Castro's rule in Cuba but it is doubtful if the United States felt the same way.

Political change takes place most peacefully in those political systems that are characterized by a high degree of consensus, where political institutions function effectively in harmony with the wishes of most people, and in tune with prevalent ideologies. While ideologies exist partly to legitimize the status quo, they also have as their *raison d'être* the accommodation of change. Thus it is not how long a regime lasts that matters but the manner of its passing: if the ruling ideology can countenance political change, such change will be of the evolutionary variety avoiding the abrupt breaks with the past that marked the end of the Weimar Republic in Germany or Portugal's departure from Angola.

Much will depend on how people view their own political system, how they rate its performance, and how involved they feel in its functioning. The sum total of these values, beliefs and emotions is sometimes referred to as the 'political culture'. Two pioneers in researching political culture defined it as 'specifically political orientations, the attitudes towards the political system and its various parts, and the role of the self in the system. The political culture of a nation is the particular distribution of the patterns of orientation towards political objects' (Almond and Verba 1963) or simply how people feel and think about a political system and its component parts. It is possible to categorize political cultures in a number of ways: to ask, for example, how likely it is that the military will intervene in politics; to ask how involved citizens feel in the decision-making process of their state; to ask whether the culture is marked by consensus or conflict. Analytically, we can distinguish between at least three components in any political culture: its cognitive, affective and evaluative aspects. Put more simply, we can ask three questions of any political system: How much do people know about it? How far do they identify with it? And how effective do they think it is? In theory, these aspects may not be positively correlated with each other. An individual may know a great deal about his own political system but he may, at the same time, feel alienated from it while conceding that it is very effective in achieving its objectives.

Clearly, a political culture is not static. As political changes take place, the collective view of the system and its constituent elements will alter. The more sweeping the changes, the more likely it is that the older generations will hold on to beliefs and assumptions that contrast with those born more recently. In West Germany, for example, it is possible to speak of a new political culture, sometimes referred to as 'post-materialism', that has become the intellectual property of a younger generation, born since the Second World War, and less concerned than its parents with the mindless pursuit of affluence. But if the political culture is prone to evolve from one generation to the next, it is also true that it varies between regions of the same country at any particular time. Sub-cultures within broader national cultures are often the result of historical developments (e.g.

2

the French settlement of Quebec) or economic forces (e.g. the increasing influx of Mexicans into California). But in a country with differential levels of economic development or poor communications, contrasting views on the political system and its effectiveness may persist. In Ireland, for example, a noticeable east–west 'gradient' exists in the political culture resulting in more liberal views on many religious and moral issues in the east of the country than in the west. In a much larger country like the United States, variations in political culture are tied more to ethnicity than strictly to geographical region although it is possible to detect a more conservative strain of politics in the Deep South.

Ethnicity, socio-economic differences, geographical 'barriers' and poor communications provide some of the factors that go to make up a heterogeneous political culture where significant groups of the population exhibit loyalties and make assumptions about the political process that are at variance with the dominant culture. The stability of a political system and the likelihood of it being able to accommodate change are closely related to the political culture and particularly to the extent to which sub-cultures are recognized, tolerated, and incorporated into the broader political system.

Spain: the land and the people

Spain is the larger of two countries that share the Iberian Peninsula. With an area of 504,800 square kilometres, it is the second most extensive state in the terms of territory in the European Economic Community. The relative isolation of any peninsular country is reinforced, in the case of Spain, by the Pyrenees running south-eastwards from the Bay of Biscay to the Mediterranean, and effectively barricading the country off from the rest of Europe. The old aphorism 'Africa begins at the Pyrenees' reflected the cultural discontinuity marked by this natural barrier, but today motorways across the frontier and political change in Spain itself, to say nothing of Spain's accession to the European Economic Community in 1986, have combined to reduce this sense of isolation.

Within Spain, geography has been the foe of those who sought to keep the reins of political power in one place. Giant rivers like the Guadalquivir and Ebro snake across the landscape marking out regions of cultural and economic diversity. The country is one of the most mountainous in Western Europe with obvious implications for effective communications and personal mobility. Madrid is the highest capital city in Europe, standing 2,100 feet above sea level, and surrounded on all sides by cordilleras that physically shield the seat

3

of government from the country it serves. Major centres of industry, like Bilbao and Barcelona, lie on the country's periphery and function as effective poles of counter attraction to the centre. Spain consists of three distinct climatic zones: the north and east enjoy a coastal climate without severe extremes of temperature and some rainfall; the central meseta experiences the greater variations of cold and heat of a continental climate and low rainfall; and the mountain zones (areas over 9,000 feet) exhibit the conditions associated with an alpine region.

The population of Spain is about 37 million people, making it the fifth most populous country in the EEC, but the density of population at 74 per square kilometre makes it relatively under-populated by general West European standards. However, there are wide variations in population density as migration from the rural south and west has tended to drift north-eastwards to the more industrialized areas as well as into Madrid itself. Thus about two-thirds of Spain's population live in one-third of its area. The people of Spain are relatively homogeneous, almost all being Roman Catholic and all being able to speak Spanish, although the Basques and Catalans and, to a lesser extent the Galicians, provide important linguistic exceptions. Even in these regions, where the non-indigenous population is significant, Spanish is universally understood and is spoken naturally by the majority of the inhabitants. Migration has been strongly driven by the search for better economic opportunities: in the 1960s, a period of rapid industrialization, more than three million people migrated from the north-west, west, and south, to the cities of the Basque country, Catalonia, and the region around Madrid.

The 'economically active' population represents about 35 per cent of the total and this proportion has remained fairly constant since about 1800. However, those in agricultural occupations now make up about 15 per cent of the total, whereas, up until about the 1950s, as much as half of those in employment were working on the land. Industrial occupations have accounted for about a third of the population since 1950, while the great expansion has been in the services, up from 27 per cent in 1960 to 52 per cent in 1985. Unemployment has become a serious problem since the early 1970s. In the mid-1980s, unemployment remained stubbornly at over 20 per cent of the working population and government policies, such as restructuring overmanned industries like steel, have if anything exacerbated the problem.

The economy

The European Economic Community provides an appropriate yardstick for a discussion of the main features of the Spanish economy. Spain is still one of the less developed members of the Community, its GNP per capita being slightly above that of Greece but less than half that of either France, West Germany, or the Netherlands. An obvious comparison can be made between Spain and Italy although contrasts between rich and poor regions are not as great in the former as in the latter. The 'economically active' population is a smaller proportion of the total population than is the case in any other EEC country; and women constitute a smaller share, 17 per cent of the workforce, than in other countries except Greece and Ireland although this situation is changing quickly. Unemployment is likely to remain a problem because the population is more youthful – only Ireland has a larger percentage of its population under the age of 15 (30 per cent to Spain's 26 per cent with the EEC average being 21 per cent).

Agriculture occupies about 18 per cent of the working population, industry 36 per cent, and services 45 per cent (as compared with EEC averages of 8 per cent, 37 per cent, and 55 per cent respectively). Thus Spain is still an important agricultural producer and is reckoned to be virtually self-sufficient in all essential commodities. Forty-one per cent of Spain's land area is arable, with grain, olive oil, and wine being the most important products. The dry climate keeps productivity low by EEC standards, and extending irrigation thus offers the best hope of raising agricultural productivity in the medium term (about 14 per cent of cultivated land is irrigated at present). Farm size varies enormously from the vast latifundia of the south to the minifundia of Galicia in the north-west. The average farm size is 19 hectares. These latifundia could be more productive if better managed: at the moment they suffer from absentee ownership and backward agricultural techniques that result in low yields. Citrus fruits have become an important Spanish export and about 3 per cent of all arable land is devoted to fruit production. Other products include olive oil, of which Spain is responsible for 40 per cent of the world's production, cotton, tobacco, and sugar beet. The dry climate means that pasture is in short supply and this in turn leaves Spain having to supplement its beef and lamb production with imports from more temperate climates. Fishing, by contrast, is an expanding industry and the Spanish fishing fleet is one of the biggest in the world, dwarfing those of her EEC neighbours. The fishing industry is centred on the northern coast and about two-thirds of Spain's fish canning industry is located in Galicia.

Wine is an important source of export revenue, with the United Kingdom accounting for around half of all Spanish exports although stiff competition for the British palate is being mounted by both West Germany and France. Following a world trend towards white and lighter wines, Spain has been adapting its techniques away from the traditionally 'robust' reds. Sherry is not often drunk in Spain itself but it makes up about a quarter of wine exports, most of it going to Britain.

Spain's industrial sector has inherited problems from the past: an anti-entrepreneurial ethos in Spanish society; lack of government initiative; lack of investment; and dependence on foreign technology. Spain became industrialized later than most West European countries due to lack of commercial enterprise, technological backwardness, low capital investment, and the small population failing to create consumer demand. Foreign wars, the war against France (1808–14), and the loss of the Spanish-American empire (1810–20) combined to avert industrial development just at the moment of its embryonic formation. Dependence on colonial possessions for raw materials and markets had led to a mood of complacency from which, once it was shattered, it was painfully slow to recuperate. Only in the twentieth century, under Franco's rule, did the State become heavily involved in industrial development and, even then, doctrinaire notions of self-sufficiency, and the cosy intimacy between capitalism and the state, contributed to clumsy and uneven advances in the industrial sector. The aim behind economic autarky had been to minimize any dependence on imports and discourage investment from abroad. Sheltered from international competition by high tariff walls, many sectors of Spanish industry have found the transition to freer trade in the post-Franco era an uncomfortable experience.

The State's role in the economy was formalized in 1941 by the creation of the Instituto Nacional de Industria (INI). Its declared objectives were to foster industrial development and promote self-sufficiency, particularly with regard to industries with a defence implication. Through much of its history the INI did not encourage industrial efficiency, but preferred to featherbed those firms who were unable to withstand the growing competitiveness of foreign firms when tariffs were eventually lowered in the 1960s.

In the 1980s the INI's role has been adapted to new circumstances. In 1982 the INI had 217,000 employees, taking in 7 per cent of Spain's industrial labour force and generating sales of over $10 billion a year, about a third of which is accounted for by exports. The INI group was responsible for all Spain's aircraft production, 80 per cent of its shipbuilding, 50 per cent of its coal, 40 per cent of its fertilizers and a third of its steel and electricity. Current policy is steadily to reduce annual losses of over $1 billion and make INI profitable. Losses are concentrated in a handful of sectors like steel and shipbuilding and in Iberia, the national airline. Firms are being sold off or shut down, and foreign multinationals are being allowed to take over subsidiaries of Spanish companies where foreign technology or marketing know-how could be beneficial. Among the two most notable sales have been of a ball-bearing subsidiary to the Swedish firm SKF, and of a controlling stake in SEAT to Volkswagen. The bulk of INI will remain intact and the plan is to make it profitable by allowing it no longer to be a refuge for 'lame duck' industries. The INI is not the only state holding company: since 1981 the Instituto Nacional de Hidrocarburos (INH) has operated in the oil and gas sector. INH participates in 52 companies and provides employment for 20,000 people. It accounts for 30 per cent of Spain's domestic energy requirements.

As Spain adapts to its membership of the EEC, there are a number of problems in the economy that will have to be overcome if the benefits of entry are to be fully exploited. Although the country has had a healthy surplus with the EEC in the past, this will no longer be the case as Spain's industry faces the gradual dismantling of tariffs that had for so long offered protection to uncompetitive industries. Inflation, fuelled partly by excessive wage levels, and partly by public expenditure, threatens to eat into the advantages that the restructuring of industry may yield. If the government can curb inflation, running at about 8 to 10 per cent, Spain could be in a strong position, in some industries, to take on any competition offered by other EEC countries. In car manufacturing, for example, the General Motors assembly plant in Zaragoza and the Ford factory in Valencia are able to compete with the best in Western Europe. The Ford plant exports 70 per cent of its production.

Unemployment, the inevitable result of the government's determined efforts to make industry more efficient, is one of the great social problems in Spain today. It has grown inexorably from 11 per cent in 1980 to 22 per cent in 1988, while the EEC average moved from around 6 per cent to 10 per cent in the same period. Youth unemployment, a blight on many West European societies, is endemic in Spain. About 50 per cent of those under the age of 25 are looking for work, more than three times the rate in other age groups. Female unemployment has risen more quickly than among males and is now 20 per cent higher. This is due to the growing participation of females in the labour force and a slight decline in the male rate. The harshness of the unemployment figures is mitigated only by the fact that they disguise a certain amount of work in the 'black economy' – the government estimates that about a million people hold jobs unofficially. For people under 25, still looking for their first job, there is the consolation that families are still traditionally a reliable source of food and shelter. Long-term unemployment (i.e. without work for more than a year) is also on the increase, representing 22 per cent of all unemployed people while those out of work for more than two years represent 35 per cent of the unemployed. As one might expect, there are regional variations in unemployment: Andalucía has a rate of about 30 per cent, and Rioja only 17 per cent. Unemployment does not afflict the less developed parts of the country disproportionately: in fact, it is in industry and in services, rather than in agriculture, that the rise in unemployment has been most keenly felt.

As in other parts of Western Europe the labour force is growing rather rapidly. In Spain this is due partly to the 'baby boom' of the newly affluent 1960s and partly to the drying up of emigration to other countries that can no longer absorb Spain's surplus labour. Even so, Spain has the lowest participation rate in the labour force of any OECD country (55 per cent in 1985) although this can be partly explained by the exceptionally low participation by females, something which is now quickly changing as women abandon traditional roles in the home, and seek both educational qualifications and work on the same terms as men. Participation rates in the oldest age cohorts are declining, however, due to more comprehensive pension eligibility, early retirement schemes, and lower retirement age.

The response of the two PSOE governments to unemployment since 1982 has been marked by a variety of evasive strategies but very little direct attempt to create the 800,000 jobs promised in the 1982 election campaign. Severe restructuring of Spain's overmanned industries has been accompanied by repeated assertions that 'there is no alternative'. On television, Gonzalez told Spanish viewers that the Government was open to dialogue but that if in the course of dialogue it was suggested that the Government should change its policy, then the dialogue would become unacceptable! The problem of unemployment is widely accepted by all the political parties as being the country's worst economic problem; but it is acknowledged by everyone, including the Government, that nothing can directly be done to tackle the problem: thus the Government engages in creating what it claims are the conditions in which job vacancies will become more numerous. The labour market has become more flexible as a result of government action to make temporary employment easier to obtain. Similarly, a scheme like the British Enterprise Zones has been launched by the Spanish government, called Urgent Re-industrialization Zones (ZUR) but these, like their British counterparts, have been long on publicity but short on job creation. Another tactic has been to 'massage' the unemployment figures: for example in 1984, a government proposal to remove everyone over 55, and all students looking for their first job, from the unemployment statistics was leaked before it could become a serious legislative proposal. Although the unemployment figures have remained stubbornly high, they would be even higher if it were not for the Government turning something of a blind eye to the 'black economy'. By definition difficult to quantify, the black economy is reckoned to account for a quarter of the building industry, a fifth of manufacturing industry, and about 18 per cent of the retail and wholesale trade plus the restaurant and hotel industries (*El Pais*, 5 May 1985).

The supreme irony of the Socialist's handling of the economy is that they came to power in 1982 on a promise of 'change', but once in power, they governed as a right-wing party would have done: they devalued the peseta, froze wages, and took steps to cut back on public expenditure. The transformation may have been due in part to a desire to reassure big business that a Socialist administration could be 'trusted with the economy', and in part to the failure of the French Socialists to achieve any progress with their electoral promises. The fight against inflation became the top priority and attention was diverted from the continuing high unemployment. One result of the PSOE's conversion to financial orthodoxy is that they have come to occupy the same electoral ground as the parties that preceded them in office, leaving the political space on their left virtually unoccupied in the absence of any real challenge from the Communists (PCE). It is probably not surprising that the fight, so far as there is a fight, against the Government's economic policies, has been waged by the trade unions of which the most important is the UGT.

No discussion of the Spanish economy would be complete without considering the banking sector. The banks in Spain have traditionally played a major role in investment in all sectors of the economy. Seven banks control 80 per cent of all commercial bank deposits: Central, Banesto, Bilbao, Hispano Americano, Santander, Vizcaya and Popular. By world standards, the banks are small fry: only the Central Bank manages to squeeze into the top one hundred banks of the world. However, the banks are able to exert a significant influence on economic and even political events if they succeed in speaking with one voice: for example, a collective endorsement from the seven banks of the Government's position on the eve of the NATO referendum carried considerable weight. More often, however, the banks are rivals, vying with each other for commercial advantage, and often dissipating their influence on divergent political goals. Their power is reflected in the fact that although there is no love lost between them and the PSOE government (none of the seven banks endorsed the PSOE in the 1982 election) the Government has not nationalized them because the PSOE, like any major party, needs finance for political campaigns. Spanish banks own vast retail networks: there is one bank branch for every 2,330 Spaniards, as compared with one for every 3,790 Britons, or 5,500 Frenchmen. Since 1978, foreign banks have been allowed a limited penetration, of just three branches, into the Spanish system, but after 1992, when financial services become liberalized throughout the EEC, there will be no limit to the expansion of foreign banks in Spain. Already some Spanish banks are finding their shares being bought up by foreigners: the Banco Popular has 30 per cent of its shares in foreign hands. To withstand the competition, some of the 'big seven' may merge; and all will have to become more efficient, more consumer-oriented, more flexible. It is likely, however, that banks will continue to play a major role in the economy, owning large segments of industry and commerce, and exerting an indefinable but decisive influence on political life.

Can 'democracy' persist?

As recently as August 1987, a British newspaper was able to comment on the fragility of Spanish democracy. 'Fear of a breakdown of democratic institutions continues to overshadow political life ... Spaniards are uneasily aware that tolerance has never been a national characteristic' (*The Sunday Times*, 30 August 1987). Whether the democratic system of government under its constitutional monarch will survive can be regarded as a key question in any assessment of political change in Spain. Answering such a question means we have to consider the basic conditions in which any liberal democracy is likely to persist; we need to identify what threats are posed to the democratic system; and finally we must ask how much popular support underpins the constitutional framework of Spanish politics.

The political system presided over by Franco for forty years can be regarded as both paternalistic and authoritarian. Franco saw himself justified by God and history: he believed he had a divine mission to save Spain from its enemies. As the coinage of the regime proclaimed, he was the caudillo 'by the grace of God'. Franco's rule lasted as long as it did because nearly a million people had died in a civil war preceding it, and no-one was prepared to risk that kind of bloodshed again. 'It survived because a determined minority wanted it to survive ... and the rest of the population was either coerced into accepting it or else prevented from doing anything that could conceivably be regarded as a threat to its existence' (Gilmour 1986: 24). Franco believed that he was defending 'real' liberties such as worship, the family, and law and order against the 'pseudo-liberties' of strikes, trade unionism and political parties. The Franco regime was also undoubtedly given an extra lease of life by the economic uplift provided by both American economic aid (following the 1953 agreement on military bases) and the general upswing in world trade in the 1960s from which Spain, like the rest of Western Europe, could not help but benefit. There followed the peculiar juxtaposition of a modernizing economy and an authoritarian political system. The latter hardly changed in the forty years of Franco's rule; but the economic autarky of the 1940s and 1950s soon gave way to the 'indicative planning' of the 1960s, shepherded along by technocrats whose success in giving Spain the developed world's fastest growth rate (outside of Japan) was used by the government to justify, and lend legitimacy to, the continued authoritarian style of rule. One effect of the Spanish *Wirtschaftswunder* was the growing gap between rural and urban areas as landless peasants flocked into the large cities to search for work; and at the same time a growing gap between rich and poor was unmitigated by any attempt at a redistribution of wealth or the creation of a welfare state. Many went abroad to take jobs in West Germany and France, and their remittances to their families, added to the income from booming tourism, were further stimulants to the economy. The middle classes were now prosperous to an extent undreamt of a generation previously, and while the regime hoped that the acquisition of cars, television sets and better housing would simply neutralize political discontent in a class that was becoming better educated, more travelled and more critical, the opposite happened. The censor continued to be active; and the media fed the people a steady diet of football matches, soap operas (with much of the 'spice' removed by the censor) and radio plays that enjoyed a phenomenal vogue in the 1960s. It has been called the 'evasion culture' because it served to wrap the critical faculties of the citizenry in the cotton wool make-believe world of Hollywood cinema.

Beneath the surface, however, two groups were beginning to agitate: students whose growing numbers formed a critical elite in Spanish society, and the workers in the large factories who were now more militant in the pursuit of pay claims. A higher standard of living, coupled with an unprecedented exposure to foreign books, films, and holidays, led to higher political expectations. Thus the economic success of the regime led not to a growing acceptance of its political basis but rather to a greater questioning of its assumptions. Women began to seek jobs that matched their recently acquired educational qualifications; and pressure from women to play a more public role in Spanish society challenged the traditional view, supported by the Church, that the primary female functions were to be a mother and a wife, but not a breadwinner. In sum, then, the economic modernization of Spain preceded its political modernization and helped to lay the foundations for it. The political butterfly was to emerge from the economic caterpillar.

While it may be easy to see the prosperity of Franco's last years as providing the springboard from which the transformation to a democratic society could be launched, there are problems in finding an easy explanation for the resilience of democracy in the post-1977 period. Conventional theories of democracy argue that a stable democracy is based on two prerequisites: first, persistent allegiance to political institutions whose effectiveness earns them legitimacy and, second, an adequate level of material well-being fairly distributed. Such an approach is borne out by the experience of liberal democracy in West Germany since 1949. At the outset, the historical precedents for the German democracy were distinctly unpromising and the early evolution of West German political institutions was greeted with a certain amount of apathy and cynicism. However, in the wake of spectacular economic success, the democratic institutions earned a legitimacy that had earlier been denied them. The temporary revival of a neo-Nazi party in 1968–9, during a brief recession in West Germany's economic fortunes, seemed to lend credence to this notion that the democratic system had been largely nourished on a diet of economic success. Today, with the institutions well established and accepted as legitimate, it would be possible for the Federal Republic to withstand an economic recession without reverting to a more authoritarian style of politics. The evidence for that argument appears in recent research on Costa Rica, a country long regarded as the epitome of liberal democracy in a region where it is a scarce commodity (Seligson and Muller 1987). Since 1982, Costa Rica has been plunged into serious economic crisis brought on by the rapid devaluation of its currency, the international debt crisis, and unfavourable terms of trade. However, support for the country's democratic system has not wavered in the shadow of economic catastrophe. The lesson to be drawn from this case is that liberal democratic values once established are not easily eroded; the danger is in trying to establish or maintain democracy prior to these values having taken root.

In the light of the foregoing argument, Spain's situation since 1977 cannot be seen as providing either of the two basic prerequisites for the establishment of democracy. In the first place, there was no sustained previous experience of democracy from which a firm attachment to liberal democratic values could have been gained; and second, there was an economic recession whose effects were to make unflattering comparisons with the 1960s and early 1970s plausible, and the task of winning the allegiance of the middle classes to the new institutions all the more difficult. Public opinion was becoming demonstrably less optimistic about the country's economic prospects. While 20 per cent of Spaniards were reported in 1976 to believe that the economy had improved over the previous year, only 7 per cent thought so in 1981 (Lopez-Pintor 1982: 37). Likewise, optimism about the country's future economic prospects declined from the 40 per cent who thought they would get 'better' in 1975 (the year of Franco's death) to the 15 per cent who thought so in 1982. There are numerous indicators of the economic crisis that hit Spain at the moment when the new democracy was first seeing the light of day. Unemployment rose from 3.8 per cent in 1975 to 7.5 per cent in 1978 and to 12.6 per cent in 1980. The distribution of income between regions had become more lopsided as a result of the economic expansion of the 1970s; and inequalities of wealth between social classes had also been exacerbated. In the 1970s the poorest 20 per cent of the population had only 5 per cent of the total income, while the richest 20 per cent had 52 per cent. Wealth distribution was twice as unequal in Spain as in Britain, Sweden or The Netherlands (Maravall 1982: 124). Maravall argues that rising prosperity once halted, coupled with acute inequalities and high unemployment, produced intense upward pressure for reform. This outweighed to some degree the political apathy, cynicism and alienation that collectively constituted the legacy of the Franco period.

The fact that faith in the democratic system was not more severely shaken by the economic crisis that engulfed it in the late 1970s can be explained partly by its evident legitimacy, and partly by the self-interest of principal actors in the political system. The role of political leaders in guaranteeing the orderly transition to democracy has been emphasized by the authors of a recent study who argue that 'the configuration of partisan forces in a new democratic system . . . is the product'of the perceptions, values, calculations, strategies, and behavior of political elites as they attempt to attract electoral support' (Gunther *et al.* 1986: 3). Specifically, the precise shape of the party system as it emerged in 1982 was, according to these authors, the product of the success, or otherwise, of party leaders in dealing with intraparty tensions in the pre-election period (Gunther *et al.* 1986: 402). In fact, no party before 1982 had either sufficiently stable support or the internal cohesion to take the necessarily harsh measures to deal with Spain's key economic problems: inflation and unemployment. The need to make political compromises, in order to effect a smooth transition towards democracy, ruled out any serious fight against the growing economic crisis since any measures would have aroused opposition in one or more of the very sectors of society on which the fragile transformation depended. As the trade union movement regained its long-lost bargaining rights, upward pressure on wage levels was difficult to resist; and as firms found their labour costs rising they raised prices thus adding to the inflationary spiral. The levels of investment fluctuated with the political uncertainty: the business community was not willing to risk capital until the political system stabilized. Normally a democratic system with only a couple of years' experience to prove itself might have been vulnerable to falling levels of support in a time of crisis. However, there is some evidence that support for democracy was already strong enough some years previous to Franco's demise to guarantee a reservoir of goodwill that could be tapped when democratic institutions were under pressure in the 1980s. When asked to choose between 'one-man government' and 'democratic representative' government at various intervals, Spanish respondents displayed a growing preference for democracy well before the dictator died. In 1966, nine years before Franco's death, those preferring democracy outnumbered those who did not by three to one; and in 1976, a year after his death, those preferring democracy were nearly ten times as numerous as those who did not (Lopez-Pintor 1982: 84).

The support for democratic institutions well before these were established, was reinforced by a high degree of self-interest on the part of the new middle class and the main political parties. The fear of a return to the Civil War, and the familiarity with stability under Franco, led to a cautious desire to reconcile the Right with the Left, and the past with the future. Public opinion overwhelmingly supported gradual change in the late 1970s, and the economic advances made under Franco by the expanding middle classes created an inbuilt political ballast to the system that instinctively excluded both radicalism and extremism. The evident pessimism about the country's economic prospects served only to underline this caution; and this in turn rebounded favourably on those politicians who were not prepared to 'rock the boat'.

The transition to democracy can be regarded as the triumph of modernity over tradition (Pollack and Hunter 1987). If the civil war had witnessed the victory of tradition over modernity, too much had happened since to allow that to happen again. The economy had become industrialized and penetrated by multinationals; tourism had imported new values and new wealth; and even the Church had begun to display a reforming face. Well before the end of the Franco period, the 'seeds of anti-authoritarianism had been securely planted' by a coalition of workers, trade unions, the intelligentsia, and technocrats in the Falange impatient to modernize the Spanish economy and pave the way for inevitable democracy (Pollack and

Hunter 1987: 359). This view that Franco's dictatorship became delegitimized by internal and external forces beyond its control is also asserted by Penniman and Mujal Leon (1985) although they, like Maravall (1982), emphasize the remarkable continuity in voting patterns between the 1930s and the 1970s.

The extent to which democratic norms had become accepted by the early 1980s is reflected in the changing roles of both the police and the Army in Spanish society. The role of the police, in any society, is arguably a reliable barometer of the relationship between the state itself and its constituent society. Attitudes towards the police can be taken as an index of the state's legitimacy (Brewer *et al.* 1988). The degree of militarization of police forces, the possibilities of policing by consent rather than coercion, collectively illustrate how the state is perceived by the public. Part of the legacy bestowed by Franco on his successors were the civil service, the judiciary and the police. It would never have been practical to 're-stock' these great agencies of the state with new men, loyal to the new political ethos; and instead, the delicate process of imbuing long established institutions with new ideas had to be set in motion. In the case of Spain's police forces, the transition was inevitably a faltering one since the very groups who under Franco had been banned, or were the object of police persecution, now had equal rights under the law. The law itself changed rapidly, allowing people to do all kinds of things which under Franco's rule would have been severely dealt with by the police: watching pornographic films; running strip clubs; bathing topless; joining a trade union; standing for the communist party in an election; flying the Basque flag; smoking cannabis.

The two principal police forces in Spain are the Policía Nacional and the Guardia Civil. The Policía Nacional is the heir to the Policía Armada which in Franco's time dealt severely with political demonstrations in the cities. Under the democratic regime, the uniforms were changed from grey to brown and the word 'Armada' was dropped. The change in image marked a transformation of function: the police are required under the 1978 Constitution to 'protect the free exercise of rights and liberties and to guarantee the safety of citizens', a very different role from that assumed in the Franco period.

Complementing the Policía Nacional, and in many respects a contrast to it, is the Guardia Civil whose distinctive uniform has hardly changed since the force's foundation in 1844. The Guardia Civil has long traditions, and is more independent than other police forces: its various functions, military, security and fiscal, mean that it is answerable to three different government ministries. It functions principally in rural areas and in towns of less than 20,000 population.

Its national responsibilities include, among other things, arms and explosives, inter-urban communications, coasts, frontiers, airports, the prevention of smuggling, the protection of public buildings, and prisons. The Guardia Civil has a tradition of being apart from the people, emphasized by members of the force living with their families in separate barracks, and recruits coming largely from the families of serving Guardia Civil personnel. In addition to the Policía Nacional and the Guardia Civil, there are the Policía Municipal whose responsibilities include traffic regulation, street markets, demonstrations and the protection of municipal buildings. In the autonomous regions like the Basque country and Catalonia, a new layer of police force has been inserted and this sometimes replaces, and sometimes complements, the functions of the two main national police forces already described. However, the multiplicity of police forces in Spain undoubtedly leads to duplication of effort, overlapping competences, rivalries and inefficiency.

On the other hand, the identification of the citizen with the police is one of the more encouraging developments of the post-Franco period. While co-operation with police in the tracking down of criminals has increased, there is also less toleration of police abuses. There have been several notorious cases of police brutality under the democratic regime, but the extent to which these have been exposed, investigated, and condemned, point to a healthier relationship between police and public reflecting a more open political atmosphere. The existence of special legislation to deal with terrorism has led to allegations that the Guardia Civil have abused the right to detain suspects without trial by ill-treating and torturing them while in custody. At the end of 1986, the Association for Human Rights in Spain reported that twenty-five members of the civil guard and police had been convicted for acts of torture, ill treatment or injuries to prisoners during the year. About 150 further trials on similar charges were pending. In November of the same year, three civil guards were imprisoned for the torture, three years earlier, of the three Olarra brothers. Of all detainees held incommunicado in 1986, about 30 per cent were actually charged, and most of these were related to the Basque separatist movement ETA (Amnesty International 1987). The Spanish government is publicly committed to the upholding of human rights, the physical and moral integrity of the person is protected by Article 15 of the Constitution, and Spain is a signatory of the European Convention on Human Rights. Nevertheless, the Government feels that the threat of terrorism permits the existence of special legislation of a type found in other West European democracies. The litmus test of Spain's commitment to the idea that the police are not above the law is the rigour with which accusations made against them are investigated.

Rising crime rates have been variously attributed to the increasing availability of, and tolerant attitudes towards, drugs; the more permissive climate in Spanish society; and the greater readiness of citizens to report crimes to the police. Whatever the reason, the crime wave in Spain is one of the top priorities for government attention, and one of the greatest threats to the country's buoyant tourist industry. The court system is creaking under the load of cases. Public opinion appears to be supportive of the police in the new democratic era. In a poll in 1983, 69 per cent and 67 per cent, respectively, of respondents gave a favourable rating to the Policía Nacional and the Guardia Civil. Seventy-three per cent said that they had always been correctly treated by the police; and three out of four respondents felt that the security forces were at the service of all people equally (Roach and Thomaneck 1985: 251).

When we come to consider the changing role of the Army in Spanish society, we have to remember that the nearest the new democracy in Spain has come to being extinguished was the attempted coup on 23 February 1981 in which sections of the Army played a leading part. The Cortes was in the process of voting to confirm Calvo Sotelo as prime minister when a group of Guardia Civil under Lieutenant-Colonel Tejero burst into the chamber, fired shots at the ceiling and effectively took the Cortes hostage. At about the same time, General Milans del Bosch, in Valencia, declared a state of emergency in his region and put tanks on the street. In the evening Tejero telephoned Milans del Bosch and informed him of the siege in the Cortes at which the general then tried to persuade other military leaders to join the coup. Tejero made a vain attempt to bluff members of the Cortes into believing that Madrid was about to fall to advancing armies closing in from several directions, but this bluff was exposed by a member of the Cortes who, hearing the reality of the situation on his transistor radio, relayed it to his colleagues. In fact, King Juan Carlos had quickly taken charge of the situation and a meeting of the joint chiefs of staff went into almost continuous session in a hotel opposite the Cortes. The King ordered Milans del Bosch to stand down his forces and, in a midnight appeal to the Spanish people on television, confirmed that he was resisting the coup, and would defend the constitution and the parliamentary system. Tejero and his co-conspirators were arrested and taken to a nearby barracks, and the members of the Cortes were set free.

The aftermath of this crisis emphasized both the enthusiasm of the Spanish people for the stand taken by the King, and the persistence of sympathy for the attempt made by Tejero and his colleagues. On 27 February (four days after the coup attempt) one million people demonstrated in Madrid in favour of the King and the parliamentary system. Later the same year, however, 200 people were held hostage in a bank in Barcelona by gunmen demanding the release of Tejero and his supporters. The siege was ended by a commando assault and, during the ensuing police enquiries, a plot to assassinate the King was uncovered. In November, the extreme right organization Fuerza Nueva exhibited its continuing strength at a mass rally, attracting 100,000 supporters, held in Madrid on the sixth anniversary of Franco's death.

The coup attempt of 23 February was the most dangerous example of the challenge posed by the Army to the fledgling democracy, but it was not a unique occasion. In 1978, a coup attempt, code-named Operation Galaxia, coincided with a fascist rally in Madrid at a time when the King was in Mexico; and in October 1982, another coup attempt failed when it was foiled by an advance tip-off, and a number of Army officers were arrested. Since 1982, there have been no serious attempts by the Army to usurp governmental authority, but Army officers remain suspicious of a Socialist government that appears to be unable to control terrorism, and has allowed the 'sacred unity' of Spain to be jeopardized by the granting of various degrees of autonomy to Spain's regions.

The resentment of the more conservative elements in the Army has to be understood in the context of the power exercised by them under Franco. One-third of all Franco's ministers were Army officers; and the Army came to see itself not only as the centre of political life under the dictatorship, but also the repository of the nation's honour and unity. Even in the new democracy, the Army continued to be a self-contained group in society, living apart in its own barracks, reading its own military journals, attending its own university colleges, inter-marrying to an extraordinary degree (it is estimated that 50 per cent of Army officers married the daughters of other officers). It is not surprising that since the 'transition', the Army has found it difficult to adapt to the permissiveness, the rising crime, the terrorism, the claims of the regions for autonomy, and the new laws on matters like divorce and abortion that have marked the development of Spanish society in the past decade.

The implication of the Army in a number of attempted coups before 1982 was a symptom of the rather indulgent attitude held towards the Army by the UCD government while in office. However, after 1982, with the PSOE in power with a clear majority and with the party itself not an intrinsically fragile coalition like the UCD, a more robust policy towards the Army could be pursued, although it is easy to forget that the reforms sustained by the new defence minister, Narcis Serra, were based on similar reforms already set in train by his

UCD predecessor Mellado. The ambition of the PSOE government has been to reduce the size of the Army by about 30 per cent by the year 2000. This is being achieved partly by reducing the period of service for conscripts, and partly by pensioning off a quarter of the Army's senior officers. There were no fewer than 404 generals on active duty in 1981; the plan was to have got rid of all of them by 1988 (Lancaster and Prevost 1985: 115). Whereas, under Franco, a massive army could have been justified by the constant need to quell signs of internal unrest, the requirements of external defence take precedence in the 1980s, but even these are fairly minimal. There are two perceived sources of external threat: one is a Warsaw Pact invasion of the Iberian Peninsula across the Pyrenees, and the other is a risk of an intrusion into Spain's two possessions in North Africa: Ceuta and Melilla. Neither can be said to be imminent threats, but the redeployment of the Spanish Army in the 1980s is a reflection of these new priorities. Mountain divisions are based near the Pyrenees, and other divisions have been spread through Andalucía to facilitate a quick transfer to North Africa if necessary. The Legion, like its French counterpart a haven for foreign mavericks whose past is not too closely probed, has long been regarded as one of the more reactionary elements in the Spanish Army: its regiments have been suitably dispersed to Fuerteventura and North Africa. Meanwhile, reserve troops for possible dispatch to the European Central Front (under NATO obligations) are headquartered at Madrid and Valencia. In an effort to reduce Spain's dependence on foreign suppliers, particularly the United States, the PSOE government has actively encouraged the Spanish arms industry. Rockets and missiles are being manufactured, some for export, and a new aircraft carrier has been built to replace an ageing ex-US Navy vessel dating from the 1940s. The Spanish Air Force is, however, still heavily dependent on American-made aircraft.

Contrary to what one might expect, the rapid transformation of Spain into a democratic political system has not fired the Spanish people with a fervent interest in politics. The efforts of the Franco regime to marginalize public opinion, and minimize political participation, seem to have carried over into the democratic era. Although in comparison with other West European societies, the Spanish seem well pleased with the performance of their own democratic institutions, this satisfaction is not translated into positive enthusiasm for either national or international politics. In late 1986, 56 per cent of Spaniards reported that they were either 'very satisfied' or 'fairly satisfied' with the way democracy works in their country. This figure compares with an average of 52 per cent in the EEC, and comes well ahead of Italy (25 per cent) and Ireland (44 per

cent) and not a long way behind the country that is most satisfied with
its democratic institutions, West Germany (71 per cent). Support for
gradual change remains very strong in Spain with both right-wing
and left-wing extremism relegated to the political sidelines. When
asked to choose between three scenarios: 'radical change by revolutionary action' or 'gradual improvement by reforms' or 'valiant
defence against all subversive forces' the gradual path of progress is
supported by 67 per cent of respondents, the revolutionary road by 3
per cent, and the reactionary defence of the status quo by 7 per cent
(Eurobarometer 1985, 1986). There has been such an erosion of support for the 'Spanish nation' as a concept that its only adherents are
now labelled right wing. Nor is the mood European: the Spanish
citizen identifies enemies as other people that covet his wealth or
property, and his focus of loyalty is the region. Regional identity in
all parts of Spain has been given a fillip by the constitutional possibilities successfully demonstrated by the Basque country and
Catalonia to name but two more successful examples of autonomous
government.

Spanish society is already displaying some of the symptoms of
'post-materialist' culture that has become a feature of late twentieth-
century Western Europe. There has been a marked decline in
religious devotion since the death of Franco. Forty-two per cent of
the population claimed to be 'practising Catholics' in 1976, but only
25 per cent in 1983 (Orizo 1983: 177). In the mid-1980s, according to
a trans-national mass opinion survey, 41 per cent of Spaniards were
attending church 'at least once a week', compared with 82 per cent in
Ireland, 30 per cent in France, and a West European average of 32
per cent (Harding 1986: 37). According to the same writer, Spanish
levels of church attendance lie midway between Ireland (the highest)
and Denmark (the lowest). Among younger people (aged 18–24)
church attendance is a declining habit, with 39 per cent of Spaniards
in this age group saying they 'never attend church', compared with
only 5 per cent in Ireland, 63 per cent in France, and a West
European average of 43 per cent. Belief in God remains strong, however, with 87 per cent of Spaniards believing in a deity, compared
with 95 per cent in Ireland, 58 per cent in Denmark, and a West
European average of 75 per cent (Harding 1986: 36–41). According
to various sociological studies, Spaniards are more cynical about
marriage than the British, and equally likely to agree with the view
that there ought to be 'total sexual freedom' (Lopez-Pintor 1982).

The speed with which the transition to democracy has taken place,
and the extent to which the process was stage-managed by the political parties, led inevitably to a certain malaise, particularly among
some young people who, deprived of real issues to fight for, simply

opted out of society and became *pasotas* – people who 'pass' as in a game of cards. The increasing use of hallucinogenic drugs completed the alienation of these 'dropouts' from the main stream of Spanish society.

This mood of unconcern with political matters is reflected in Spanish literature and Spanish films: the themes are escapist, fantastic, mystical, surreal, ephemeral and often despairing, and they shy away from the factual, from reality, from anything resembling a documentary approach. The film *Cria Cuervos*, for example, studies the impact of the transition to democracy on one family, and includes a scene where an aged Army general dies of a heart attack while on active service – in the bed of his mistress. This brief scene effectively encapsulates, in mocking symbolism, the passing of the old order. Feminist films and soft pornography thrive in a cultural climate that seems to be over-compensating for years of censorship and repression. In Catalonia and the Basque country the cinema reflects the regional preoccupation with ethnic identity, and pride in a separate history.

Writing in 1982, Maravall attributed the fragility of Spanish democracy to five problems: tension between the central state and peripheral nationalisms; a cynical view of politics and politicians; a serious economic crisis; social and economic inequality; and terrorism and violence. Since 1982, progress towards the mitigation of all these problems has been achieved. Indeed, given the persistence of two of these problems – in particular, terrorism and the economic crisis – it is remarkable how far Spaniards have continued to support the parliamentary process. It may be that sufficient economic progress was achieved under the last years of Franco's rule for Spanish society to have become moderate, slightly conservative, and reluctant to risk its economic achievements in either a new civil conflict or an authoritarian dictatorship. The real consensus in the Spanish party system, epitomized most forcibly by the existence of an ostensibly left-wing government following policies that seem to be right of centre, provides a signpost indicating stability in the future.

Chapter two
Political parties: a deceptive change

Introduction

In this chapter we consider the transformation of Spain's political parties since the restoration of democracy. We chart the changing fortunes of the parties in the elections of 1982, 1986 and 1987, and this provides the background for a closer analysis of the two most important and linked developments during the 1980s: the rise of the Socialists (PSOE), and the decline of the Communists (PCE). Finally, we assess the current state of the party system in Spain. However, we preface our discussion on political parties by attempting to define their role in the political system.

At its most basic, the defining activity of a political party is the pursuit of power in a political system. So universal are political parties across the different types of political system, it is hard to imagine politics without them. They exist in democracies, but also in authoritarian states; and even the totalitarian state builds its power around one party. Free competition between political parties is often considered to be an essential feature of democratic systems, but the one-party states of the Third World have laid claim to a particular brand of democracy whose credentials are always open for inspection.

Political parties perform a variety of functions within the political system. They aggregate diverse interests in political society, they simplify issues, they 'prioritize' the political issues by grouping them in order of importance. Parties also act as a bridge between the people and the government: they communicate policies downwards, they transmit demands upwards, and they recruit leaders for the system. They mobilize support for political agendas by encapsulating complex policies in slogans and party manifestos, they represent broad values in society. 'All political parties have philosophical bases, no matter how blurred and no matter how divorced from the

22

actual political behaviour of the party these foundations may be' (Ball 1983: 79).

Recent elections

The election of 28 October 1982 was the third general election since the restoration of democracy and was in fact precipitated by the collapse of the governing party, the UCD. The party can be said to have been beset both by external pressures such as terrorism and economic recession, as well as the internal stresses of a party that was little more than a coalition of diverse interests with a common concern to see democratic government evolve in a gradual way. Once the democratic system was established, even if it remained fragile, 'power proved to be only a temporary glue to bind these disparate elements together' (Marcus 1983). The fragility of the new democracy had already been amply demonstrated by the abortive coup on 23 February 1981 led by Tejero, as well as by the inability of the UCD to tackle pressing issues such as tax reform and a new divorce law. The unpopularity of the government was being registered in regional elections: in Galicia in 1981 the Alianza Popular had overshadowed the UCD; and in Andalucía, the following year, the UCD was pushed into third place with the PSOE scoring an ominously overwhelming victory. The PSOE entered the 1982 election with a deliberately moderate programme designed to attract a wide spectrum of electoral support. The tone was pragmatic: Gonzalez had jettisoned Marxist dogma in 1979, and there was little to scare the middle classes in his electoral platform. Nationalization was to be kept to a minimum; 800,000 jobs were promised; public expenditure was envisaged that would 'prime the pump' of private enterprise; and various measures would be taken to help small businesses, such as lower social security contributions from employers. The general thrust of the programme differed little from what the UCD had been trying, albeit unsuccessfully, to achieve. When the election came, many of those who had voted for the UCD now felt able to vote for the PSOE. The victory of the PSOE can be described as a landslide. With 46 per cent of the vote and 202 seats in the 350-seat Cortes, Gonzalez had an absolute majority and was the first Socialist prime minister in Spain for fifty years. The rise of the PSOE was matched by the collapse of the UCD, down from 35 per cent of the vote in 1979 to just 7 per cent in 1982. The main opposition party was now the Alianza Popular who had drawn heavily on those who had deserted the UCD in its time of trouble but had not felt able to vote for the PSOE. The Alianza's share of the vote went up from 6 per cent to 25

23

per cent and 106 seats. The party system had become more bipolar, with the Alianza and the PSOE sharing between them 308 seats and 70 per cent of the vote. At the same time the Spanish electorate had resoundingly endorsed the democratic system, since the turnout had risen from 68 per cent in 1979 to 78 per cent in 1982. The electoral system had also assisted the bipolarization of the Cortes: the PSOE had won 46 per cent of the vote but secured 58 per cent of the seats, while the Alianza won 25 per cent of the vote and secured 30 per cent of the seats.

The election marked the collapse of the communists (PCE) as much as it did of the UCD. Out of twenty-three seats they managed to retain only four. There is no doubt that many voters on the left had voted tactically for the PSOE to maximize the strength of the more credible of the two parties. The PCE itself was, in any case, hopelessly divided between the reformist element and those who wanted to stick to a pro-Soviet line. The leadership of Carrillo had unsuccessfully tried to combine these two factions in the party. The split in the national PCE was mirrored by splits in the regional Communist parties in the Basque country and in Catalonia. In the trade union movement, the PCE found itself increasingly marginalized by the UGT (Unión General de Trabajadores) which was firmly linked to the PSOE. After the election the PCE found itself ideologically stranded by the diminishing appeal of Eurocommunism, and caught in the dilemma of whether to abandon Stalinism or embrace it; and electorally occupying a vacuum where it was faced with the choice of either distancing itself from the PSOE, or pursuing the futile path of trying to outdo the PSOE in moderation. In late 1982, largely as a result of its electoral misfortunes, the PCE adopted a new leader in the person of Gerardo Iglesias, but retained Carrillo on the party's executive. In the regions, the PSOE increased its support: in Catalonia the party came out well ahead of the main regional party, the CiU; and in the Basque country, the PSOE drew level with the PNV, each taking eight seats.

The 1986 election, held on 22 June, saw another decisive victory for the PSOE, an unprecedented event in the history of Spanish socialism. With 44 per cent of the vote, the party took 184 seats in the 350-man Cortes. On the right, the Coalición Popular, made up of the Alianza with two smaller parties, took 26 per cent of the vote and 105 seats. On the extreme left, the PCE in its new guise, and the Izquierda Unida, took seven seats (4.6 per cent of the vote). In the regions, regional parties made inroads into the PSOE vote. In Catalonia, the CiU took eighteen seats (5 per cent) and in the Basque country there was a significant shift towards more radical politics with the moderate PNV losing two seats, and the more extreme groups the

HB and EE taking an extra three seats and one seat respectively. In Aragon, the Canaries, Valencia, and Galicia, nationalist parties won a seat each.

The 1986 election took place a few months earlier than had been strictly necessary. This was due almost totally to the desire of President Felipe Gonzalez to capitalize on his victory in the NATO referendum (March 1986) and to win a new mandate ahead of the tricky subsequent negotiations with the United States over the military bases. The election campaign of the PSOE followed directly from the disciplined party machine that had successfully secured Gonzalez his victory in the referendum. Using the slogan 'Por buen camino' (by the right road), the party emphasized consolidation, continuity, modernization and reform. The recent entry of Spain into the European Economic Community was exploited as a theme in itself: the need for Spain to be truly 'European' and to adapt itself to the needs of the wider family to which it now belonged. Many of the issues which had been precursors of 'change' were resurrected now in the service of 'continuity': tax reform and better educational, welfare, and health services. In government, the PSOE had shown themselves to be moderate in both policies and implementation. In the 1986 campaign they were able to reap the benefits of this, since there was little to distinguish them in practice from the centre-right coalition that was challenging them for the middle ground in Spanish politics. The 1986 election campaign was the most routine and colourless of the post-Franco period; and the electorate clearly saw the PSOE as being the best party to tackle the issues that were themselves beyond dispute. Gonzalez' refusal to engage in television debates with opposition leaders, despite his pre-eminence as a communicator on television, kept the election campaign subdued, and prevented the more blatantly unfulfilled promises of the PSOE government from being given too much air-time. In fact, the Prime Minister's refusal to debate, by becoming a campaign issue itself, only served to underline the paucity of 'real' issues. The Popular Coalition failed to make much of the Government's failures, even the failure to create 800,000 jobs. The Coalition tried to attack the style of the government but its policies were insufficiently distinctive to make much of an impact on potential PSOE 'deserters': less public expenditure, tax cuts, and modest privatization. In foreign affairs, full membership of NATO and closer ties to the USA seemed likely to be vote losers in the wake of the NATO referendum. The Coalition leader Fraga tried to dissociate himself from a Francoist past that was clearly a liability in the mid-1980s, but his own personality, and his authoritarian style, contrasted unfavourably with that of Gonzalez whose charisma had, if anything, been enhanced by four years in government and by achieving his party's volte-face on the NATO question. Fraga's electoral chances were equally undermined by the CDS, a centrist alternative to the Coalition for voters reluctant to vote for the PSOE. Suarez campaigned on his own record in office, and tried to expose the broken promises of the Gonzalez government. The offer to reduce military service to three months and the call for a more 'independent' foreign policy helped the CDS to attract votes. The party ended up with nineteen seats in the Cortes compared with two in 1982, although the vote had increased less dramatically from 2.9 per cent to 9.2 per cent in the same period. On the left, the Izquierda Unida (IU) was the hastily formed coalition of far-left groups with the PCE (under its new leader Gallego) as the linchpin. Despite the rightward drift of the PSOE in the period 1982–6, there did not seem to be any political space to occupy on the far left for either Gallego in the IU or Carrillo in his own Communist Unity party. Although the IU managed to win seven seats, Carrillo's 'rump party' failed to get a single seat.

The results of the 1986 election not only confirmed the choice the electorate had made in 1982, but emphasized further the bipolarization of the party system. The Popular Coalition and the PSOE had secured between them 70 per cent of the vote and 82 per cent of the seats. The formation of the Izquierda Unida, and of the CDS, were each a recognition of the need to avoid any unnecessary 'splintering' of the party system if the hegemony of the two major parties was to be challenged.

In 1987, the triple election held on 10 June suggested that the position of the PSOE, apparently impregnable a year previously, was now less firmly based. The year was one of troubles for the PSOE: lightning strikes by transport workers backed by the PSOE's own affiliated union movement the UGT, an alarmingly high crime rate, much of it drugs related, and a stubbornly high unemployment rate affecting about 50 per cent of those under the age of 24. Industrial action became almost endemic with air-traffic controllers, miners, farm workers, dockers and bankers being among those who used the strike weapon. In the background the continuing violence perpetrated by ETA induced a mood of despair that reflected a widespread belief that the Government was not on top of the situation. A gloomy interpretation of events could argue that a collapse of the PSOE was imminent but a more optimistic scenario was simply that the Government was reaping the harvest of its own election promises, the need to administer drastic remedies to the economy, and the inevitable impatience with a government that was beginning to become a little too sure of itself, a little too arrogant, and had not entirely escaped a whiff of corruption. The problems facing the Government in

1987 arose partly from its increasingly unresponsive attitude to its detractors, and partly from an increasing moderation that tended to alienate groups on whom it had depended for electoral support but who now felt let down by the Government's policy. In particular, the emphasis on strict monetarism, coupled with progressive social legislation, failed to satisfy demands from the unemployed and from trade unions. There had been a relaxation on the laws regarding soft drugs, abortion and divorce, but this had been balanced by a cut in corporation tax and a reduction in employers' national insurance contributions. The NATO referendum had been widely regarded as a success especially as it would entail a reduced dependence on the United States for military equipment. But while the banks welcomed anti-inflation policies, and industry welcomed the reduction in corporation tax, the trade unions remained unimpressed by the failure to tackle unemployment, and the young educated voter was disillusioned by the way in which the NATO issue had been manipulated by the Government for what appeared to be purely utilitarian purposes.

Spain's membership of the EEC had undoubtedly brought credit to the Government but economically the effects were becoming very mixed, and contributed to the problems in the economy with which the Government had to grapple. Although there had been some foreign investment, the beneficial effects of this were more than counterbalanced by a growing trade deficit with the rest of the EEC and higher inflation resulting from the introduction of VAT. The effects of the CAP were already beginning to affect agriculture, an industry that still employs 17 per cent of the labour force. Dairy farms were suffering from EEC competition as was industry: there was a 32 per cent rise in imports from the EEC during 1986. Spain was becoming more efficient in precisely those industries where the Community was already self-sufficient: shipbuilding, steel, car production, textiles, and chemicals. The advantage of lower labour costs formerly enjoyed by Spain was now being eroded by trade union militancy. An attempt by the Government to curb wage rises to 5 per cent had been challenged by the UGT despite its special relationship with the PSOE. From the viewpoint of the UGT, the Government, far from creating jobs, seemed bent on creating unemployment by its restructuring of industries like steel and shipbuilding, industries that were, moreover, strongholds of UGT support.

This dissatisfaction with the Government from what might be termed its natural supporters partly explains the rather disappointing election results for the PSOE in 1987. There was also some cynicism about the style of government, in particular the apparently cavalier attitude displayed by Gonzalez towards the Cortes: he appeared there on only one occasion in the first seven months after the 1986 election. Like others before him he had become something of a recluse in his official residence. The election results were to have the effect of inducing a mood of caution. In particular, the relationship with the UGT could not be allowed to be stretched any further. If the PSOE was to retain any semblance of credibility as a socialist party, it would have to merit the support of the UGT. As one observer wrote shortly after the elections of 1987, 'The Government stands legitimately accused of doing little that bears any ostensible relevance to the cause of socialism or the working class' (Heywood 1987).

Since the terrorism of ETA is widely perceived to be the principal threat to Spanish democratic stability in the late 1980s, there is a great deal of support by the Spanish people for measures taken by the Government against ETA. The minister of defence has earned the respect of the Army, and the threat of a military coup is now less likely than it has ever been. Manpower levels have been reduced; military regional boundaries have been redrawn; equipment has been modernized; promotion procedures have been rationalized; and above all, the Army has begun to think of itself as a professional defence force with an international role rather than as a garrison force charged with suppressing disorder within its own territory. Any successes achieved in reducing the United States military presence in Spain not only makes Spain less dependent on American weaponry for its own uses, but it also evokes a positive response from the streak of anti-Americanism that still pervades the Spanish political culture, and which is nurtured by the memory that the United States gave credibility to the Franco regime by its economic and military support.

The rise of the PSOE

The Partido Socialista Obrero Español (PSOE) was founded in 1879 and is the oldest of Spain's political parties. During the Second Republic it had been the largest party on the left but, during the Franco dictatorship, its time in exile left it virtually extinct in Spain itself. Unlike the PCE, which had maintained a vigorous opposition to the Dictator's rule, the PSOE's structure based on open branches made it much more vulnerable to police penetration than the cell-structure of the PCE. The PSOE leadership in exile lost touch with changing events in Spain so that when the party eventually returned it came back with out-of-date attitudes, as if the intervening period had been spent in a time-warp. From 1976, when the PSOE actually included the word 'Marxist' in its description of itself for the first time, up until 1979 when the party assumed a social democratic stance, the party presented itself as a radical alternative to the PCE, proposing nationalization of the largest banks and industrial firms, and rejecting any kind of compromise with a capitalist system. Despite this ideological extremism, and with Gonzalez as its main exponent, the party's image was·put across to the voters as fairly moderate. Electorally, this proved a wise ploy since the bulk of the Spanish voters could already be found just to the left of centre on the political spectrum (Maravall 1982: 22) and the success of the PSOE in the 1977 elections vindicated the strategy. Between 1977 and 1979, the view of Gonzalez that the party had to broaden its social base in order to win a majority at the next election began to win the upper hand in the party. The legalization of the PCE in 1977 had already divided the political space on the left between two parties suggesting that the PSOE should move further towards the centre. In addition, the governing UCD looked most vulnerable on its left flank and it seemed (and it was later proved to be the case) that here there were votes waiting to change horses at the next election. Participation in the Moncloa Pacts of 1977 reflected the desire of all the main parties to co-operate in the maintenance of the transition to a stable democratic system even at the expense of hurting working-class voters among whom both the PCE and PSOE purported to have their electoral base. It was largely the electoral expediency of this shift to the centre that angered the left flank of the PSOE whose opposition to the growing moderation of the party earned it the name of *críticos*. The *críticos* also deplored the apparent personality cult developing around Gonzalez, whose vote-winning capacity seemed to be accorded greater priority than socialist principles. Gonzalez eventually outwitted the *críticos* at the 1979 party congress by threatening to resign; the fact that there was no leader capable of replacing him proved decisive although the Extraordinary Congress held in September 1979 was not a complete endorsement of *felipismo*. In the period up to the 1982 elections, events reinforced the need for PSOE moderation: the attempted coup in 1981 underlined the fragility of the transition to democracy, and the collapse of the UCD opened up a tempting space in the centre of the political spectrum. By the 1982 election the PSOE was poised to become the majority party.

The shift from socialism to social democracy was a rapid one. This can be accounted for by a number of factors (Share 1985: 98), among them the fact that the PSOE membership base was very narrow: about 2 per cent of its voting strength. It therefore had to match the ideological purity of its elite with the much more moderate convictions of its voters. Second, it was bent on becoming the party of government: if the essence of a political party is to 'prevail over others in order to get into power' (Schumpeter 1961: 279), if it is 'this goal of attaining political power that distinguishes political parties from other groups in the political system' (Ball 1983: 75), then the PSOE has behaved like a true political party in the period since 1977. To have sacrificed its electoral opportunities on the altar of ideological consistency would have robbed it of its *raison d'être*. To have refused to co-operate with the UCD government in the traditional process of restoring democracy might have denied it the chance of ever benefiting from the fruits of the new system: again its whole purpose as a party might have been lost. In the 1980s the PSOE has undoubtedly lost some of its credibility as a 'socialist workers' party' (indeed its electoral successes since 1982 depend on middle-class support), but it has gained credibility as an effective party of government, and one which responds to the deep-rooted and traditionally moderate instincts of the Spanish electorate. One writer (Maravall 1982) has traced the almost uncanny continuity between the left-wing vote in the 1930s and the left-wing vote in the 1980s.

The rise of the PSOE in the period before 1982 and the parallel decline of the PCE are mirrored in the fortunes of the two trade union organizations with which the two parties are associated. The Unión General de Trabajadores (UGT) which had been founded in 1888 hardly survived the period of the Franco dictatorship. Like the PSOE it was virtually annihilated leaving the main task of working-class resistance to the PCE and the Comisiónes Obreras (CCOO). However, during the transition to democracy, the trade union elections showed a swing to the UGT. Between 1978 and 1982 the UGT increased its share of trade union members from 21 per cent to 36 per cent, while the CCOO stagnated at around 34 per cent. The co-option of the democratic process by the forces of the Right proved profoundly dispiriting for the Left and for the working class: but given the evident conservatism of the Spanish working class, this may not have been far from the main stream of public opinion. The Army posed a threat to the transition process; had it gone wrong they might have pounced. This led to caution, not only on the part of the political parties who co-operated with each other, but also on the part of the trade unions who moderated industrial action during a time of severe economic recession in order to avoid provoking military intervention. The Moncloa Pacts which proved disastrous for the industrial working class were supported not only by all the principal parties but indirectly by the two trade union groups who had little choice but to support their political protégés: the PCE and the PSOE. Unemployment rose steadily after the Pacts were signed: from 6 per cent in 1977 to 14 per cent in 1982, even though inflation was contained. The UGT joined the PSOE in 1980 in signing an agreement with the employers' organization, an agreement that effectively restricted trade union rights and limited the scope of industrial action, albeit in return for a guarantee on the part of the employers to support increases in social security payments and job creation programmes. The conservatism of the Spanish working class was reflected in opinion surveys that showed that most workers believed that workers had the most power in West Germany and France while only 4 per cent believed that this was true in the Soviet Union. 'Such a low identification with the USSR demonstrates the lack of ideological penetration into the Spanish working class' (Prevost 1984: 90). Fading perceptions of class antagonism were also revealed by the finding that fewer workers in 1980 believed that 'workers and management have nothing in common' than in 1978 (Prevost 1984: 89). The strongly-held belief among Spanish workers that trade unions should not be politicized affects the CCOO more adversely than the UGT. Unionization, at about 15 per cent of the employed population, remains one of the lowest in Western Europe. The alliance between the UGT and the PSOE during the 1980s has been one of the PSOE's main assets, because the union delivers votes at elections and lends credibility to the party's increasingly tenuous link with authentically working-class interests. Indeed, the UGT has on occasions proved to be a mixed blessing for the PSOE, since by withdrawing its support it can demonstrate the transparency of the label *obreros* in the party's title. 'However, the PSOE–UGT relationship can also become a two-edged sword. While the UGT is socialist-led, the rank-and-file workers will not necessarily go along with a government-sponsored austerity programme even from a socialist government' (Prevost 1984: 93).

If the PSOE had been criticized only for ceasing to be an authentic 'socialist' party it might have been able to ride out the storms whipped up by its opponents. However, more damaging criticisms relate to allegations that the party is no longer run in a democratic fashion, and that its decision-making is increasingly centralized. Ironically, perhaps, the same criticism that had been levelled at the PCE, that it was stifled by 'democratic centralism', was now being directed towards the PSOE.

Indeed, if we look at the distribution of power within the PSOE, we see that it is almost the exact antithesis of what the party statutes require. The two leading figures in the party, Gonzalez and Guerra his deputy, have managed to concentrate power in a 'kitchen cabinet' around them. On several occasions the party has had to ratify the decisions taken within this clique: for example, the decision to drop Marxism from the party's ideology in the late 1970s and the decision to remain in NATO in 1982. Party congresses tend to be set-piece affairs with local branches being disinclined to upset party policy as laid down by the centre. Debate centres on policy documents circulated by the leadership; and the leader's popularity discourages open challenges to his authority. Regional governments, however, provide the only real counter-attractions to the 'pull' of the central leadership. In several regions, Valencia, Catalonia and Madrid itself, party 'barons' are able to dispense their own patronage and thus build up clientelist power bases that may rival the authority of the centre. Twenty-three per cent of party members come from Andalucía and this region in particular has established itself as something of a thorn in the side of the national PSOE organization. There are a number of factors that have contributed, however, to the persistent dominance of the national leadership of the PSOE in the party. The electoral system is a list system and this enables the party leadership to determine the order of the candidates at election time and, hence, who will be elected. The appeal of the party has extended outside the traditional working-class voters to embrace the middle sectors, and Gonzalez has used his personal charisma to appeal to a number of diverse electorates. Finance provides another source of strength to the party leadership as about 90 per cent of party funding comes from the state and is therefore in the gift of the leadership. The media, and especially television, have remained under state control with the result that the PSOE leadership has been able to communicate directly with the electorate over the heads of the party membership. The advantages of a state-run television broadcasting system explain the dragging of feet over privatization of TV channels. Patronage is also an important source of central control. About 40 per cent of party members hold some kind of political office; this dependence on the leadership for emoluments stifles criticism and dilutes debates within the party. The stagnation of real debate, the apparently increasing conservatism of the PSOE, and the failure to expand party membership, have resulted in a certain cynicism and a real danger that important sectors of potential support for the party will be alienated. The young have vented their wrath in campus unrest, and the trade union movement, the UGT, has broken away effectively from the party and has instigated considerable industrial unrest. There is some evidence that the leadership is aware of growing disenchantment with their style of governing, and speeches have begun to warn of the dangers of 'oligarchization' and *oficialismo* but there is still no sign of real attempts being made to combat this sense of disillusionment. Gonzalez' personal popularity has declined since the 1986 election, despite his successes against Basque violence, due to his relatively lacklustre performance in the economic arena.

At the beginning of 1988, unemployment moved over the three million mark, and the PSOE annual congress in January was surrounded by growing impatience on the party's left wing at the lavish lifestyles of the party leadership, and the apparent unwillingness of the prime minister to tackle unemployment. What one newspaper called the 'metamorphosis of marxist revolutionaries into the ruling pseudo-socialist yuppies of today' (*The Sunday Times*, 24 January 1988) marks the embourgeoisement of a party that includes the word 'workers' in its title. Criticisms of the government include allegations that too much is being spent on trips abroad, that the president of the congress was being housed at taxpayers' expense in a £2,250-a-month dwelling, that the party was placing its own followers in positions of influence in banks and industry, and that the television channel was being used as a propaganda organ by the Government.

The decline of the PCE

The Partido Comunista de España (PCE) was born in 1920 as a result of a split in the PSOE. It was not electorally important until after the civil war when, despite the clandestine existence it was forced to lead under the Franco regime, it became the most important focus of opposition to the dictator's rule. Its experience as an underground party undoubtedly left a lasting impact on its organization and character. It was selective in its recruitment of new members, highly centralized in its decision-making, and intolerant of views that clashed with those of the party leadership. While its affiliation to the Third International left little scope for ideological debate within its ranks, there is no doubt that its clandestine activities imposed their own logic of discipline and uniformity. The shroud of secrecy that surrounded the party's struggle against Franco made an authoritarian decision-making style almost inevitable; in such a political atmosphere, to have allowed alternative points of view to be freely expressed would have dangerously weakened the party and left it wide open to infiltration by the police.

However, as the Franco era neared its end the party began to transform itself into a mass-mobilization party actively seeking a wider membership, being less selective in its recruitment and ideologically more heterogeneous. By 1975, the PCE was the biggest party political organization in Spain; and its membership swelled to around 100,000 by 1977 (the year in which it was legalized) as the prospects of participation in the electoral process became imminent. The long history of opposition that the party had maintained during the dictatorship left it with a mixed legacy for its future in democratic

33

politics. On the one hand, as the one consistent focus of anti-Franco sentiment during the previous forty years, the PCE emerged with some prestige in a political system that was trying quickly to eradicate the remnants of an authoritarian regime. The PCE had good reason to expect its record of sacrifice in the past to be rewarded now. On the other hand, the party had to contend with a strongly negative image inculcated during the Franco years. In fact, the propaganda against the PCE was so effective that it actually enhanced the party's credibility as a political force. Franco exaggerated the threat of the PCE to shore up the argument that his own regime was the bulwark against the 'red peril'. In so doing, he inadvertently boosted the confidence of PCE activists in Spain who almost became convinced of Francoist arguments that the PCE was on the verge of bringing the Falangist edifice crashing down. 'Thus, throughout the Franco dictatorship, the PCE was allowed to play a somewhat vicarious role centre-stage in a manner not open to its Socialist rivals' (Heywood 1987). There was, however, a darker side to the image of the PCE during the transitional period to democracy. Just as the civil war could be attributed in part to a plot by the Communists in 1936, so in 1977 the PCE was portrayed by its opponents as the 'wreckers', the ones whose opposition to Franco had been unconstructive, and who now hoped for a *ruptura* from Francoism not a peaceful *reforma*. Legalized only a few months before the 1977 elections, the PCE could not shake off the heavy *impedimenta* of the Franco years. Although its party programme was 'sanitized' to make it appeal to moderate voters, and attempts made both to attract Catholics to the party and to soften the activities of the Communist trade unions, the voters were not impressed. The ubiquitous presence of the PCE throughout the country, and in many affiliated organizations, could not in the event mobilize the voters in large numbers. It was clear that although the voters wanted to say farewell to Franco they were not prepared to say farewell to the Francoist analysis of the PCE.

In the 1977 election, the PCE polled only 9.4 per cent of the vote to the PSOE's 29.9 per cent, and in 1979 the party only managed a slight increase to 10.4 per cent. These performances were achieved even though the party cultivated an assiduously moderate image after 1977, touting 'Eurocommunism', dropping Leninism from the party statutes and collaborating in the Moncloa Pacts (which set wage level maxima) in October 1977. The party was soon beset by ideological disputes between the 'Eurocommunists', led by Carrillo, the pro-Soviet bloc led by Lister, and the intellectual *renovadores* who wanted a looser party structure and more ideological flexibility. By 1982, the Carrillo faction had won the upper hand, and the Lister faction had left to form a new party. At the 1982 elections the PCE was virtually obliterated, securing only 3.8 per cent of the vote. By that time, the party had become more like its French and Italian counterparts but in assuming their moderate policies under the label of Eurocommunism had simply marginalized itself in the Spanish party system and been forced into a dilemma from which it has never since escaped: whether to compete with the PSOE as a moderate party of the left or to remain strictly on the far left but risk being simply irrelevant in Spanish politics. Moreover, the ageing leadership, unique among Spanish parties in the early 1980s, was an uncomfortable reminder of the civil war in the minds of Spanish voters.

An analysis of the Spanish electorate in 1979 gives us further clues as to why the PCE was not able to become, as it expected it would, the principal party on the left during the transition to democracy (Maravall 1982). In the first place, there is evidence of considerable continuity in voting habits between the electorates of the pre-and post-Franco period despite the intervening forty-year parenthesis. In the last parliamentary elections before the dictatorship, the Socialists won 21.4 per cent of the vote and the Communists 2.9 per cent. Despite the robustness of the Communists as an opposition force during the dictatorship, and the rather dispirited performance of Socialists during the same period, the relative strengths of the two groups in post-dictatorship politics emerged unchanged. Moreover, while parental sympathies in the civil war are a reliable determinant of voters' electoral preferences in 1979, there is a greater drift from pro-Francoist parents to left wing parties than vice-versa, with the PSOE being the principal beneficiary. Thus 'the PCE received 2 per cent and the PSOE 14 per cent of votes of children of families which were pro-Francoist during the war ... the votes of children of pro-Republican families were awarded almost exclusively to the Left, above all to the PSOE, which received a proportion two and a half times greater than the PCE' (Maravall 1982: 25). The same writer has remarked on the 'competing rather than complementary' nature of the two parties' electoral attraction and, in terms of ideological self-identification, voters for the two parties place themselves on almost identical points of the political spectrum. On a five point left–right scale, PCE voters put themselves at 1.71, PSOE voters put themselves at 2.23, and the 'centrist' UCD voters saw themselves at 3.14 (incidentally much more right of centre than the PSOE was left of centre). Other analyses of the political position of the PSOE indicate 'an important ideological proximity with the PCE' (Maravall 1982: 184).

The results of the 1982 elections were little short of disastrous for the PCE. The expulsion of the *renovadores* in 1981 dealt a blow to the party's electoral prospects. A party that called itself

'Eurocommunist' and yet refused to apply the principles of internal democracy to its own organization, alienated many voters on the far left. After the election, Carrillo resigned as general secretary, and his place was taken by a close colleague, Gerardo Iglesias, whom Carrillo undoubtedly hoped would steer a similar ideological course in the future. In 1983, Iglesias was re-elected as general secretary for a three-year period, but differences between him and Carrillo had already surfaced and were developing into a split between two ideological factions: while Carrillo had now shifted towards a pro-Soviet line apparently spurning his earlier flirtation with Eurocommunism, Iglesias seemed to have moved slightly in the opposite direction, from being the 'hard man' in 1982, but now espousing the more flexible approach of Eurocommunism. The gloomy electoral prospects for the party provided scope for considerable infighting, and Iglesias now blamed Carrillo for the débâcle of 1982.

In January 1984, a new pro-Soviet communist party was launched, called Partido Comunista (PC), led by Gallego. This development not only contributed to the disunity on the far left but it further weakened the PCE by siphoning off discontented members. In December 1984 a group of 100 members of the PCE under Ballesteros left to join the PC. Amidst the ensuing recriminations, Ballesteros accused Iglesias of betraying the 'Marxist–Leninist' principles of the PCE and contributing to its downfall, while preserving within the new PC the unadulterated doctrines of communism.

Meanwhile, in the PCE, Carrillo was continuing to oppose Iglesias' policies and in particular the latter's plan to form a broad alliance of all 'progressive' groups to the left of the PSOE, the so-called Convergencía de Izquierda. Such an alliance would include all so-called 'progressive forces' in Spanish society, those who opposed Spain's membership of NATO, the Government's economic policies, and the anti-terrorist laws. Carrillo proposed an alternative programme of policies for the alliance which he wished to call a 'union of communists'. In March 1985, at a meeting of the party's central committee, Iglesias asked Carrillo to retract his earlier statement that there were really two parties within the PCE. A ten-point peace plan was offered by Iglesias to Carrillo's supporters in an attempt to patch up differences between the two factions. Among the ten points were a suggestion that extraordinary congresses should be held in two Carrillo strongholds, Madrid and Valencia, in an attempt to secure for supporters of Iglesias positions of influence within the party; and that the party newspaper *Ahora*, edited by Carrillo, should be either closed or its political stance radically altered. In October 1985, some supporters of Carrillo broke away to form their own party, the Partido Comunista de España–marxista revolucionaria (PCE–mr) while still claiming that they wanted to preserve the solidarity of the Communist movement in Spain. An attempt, later the same month, to weld the (now) three communist parties together failed when two of the three parties boycotted the proposed congress. However, in the 1986 general election the Communist parties patched up a last-minute alliance called Izquierda Unida which won seven seats in the Cortes.

What kind of party system?

So far our discussion has centred on the individual parties. Any understanding of how parties function in a political system must be considered in the context of the overall party system that operates. The most frequently used classifications of party systems refer either to the number of parties in the system or to the relative strengths of the parties. Broad distinctions can be made, therefore, between one-party systems like those of the USSR or Tanzania and two- or multi-party systems like those of the United States and Italy respectively. In two-party systems, power tends to alternate between two major parties although the existence of one or more additional smaller parties in the system is not excluded; the essential characteristic is the predominance of two parties and their capability to alternate in government. In a multi-party system, no single party is dominant, and the typical pattern is for coalitions of two or more parties in legislatures where as many as ten or twelve parties may be represented. The distinctions between these three types of system are not clear-cut since a one-party system may, or may not, allow competitive elections between rival factions within the ruling party; and in two-party systems, like West Germany or the Irish Republic, the role of a small third party may be crucial in determining which of the two major parties takes office. In multi-party systems, bipolar configurations may emerge, causing alternations in government between right and left that are reminiscent of two-party systems. Such considerations, however, bring us to consider the other type of party system: the one which takes the relative strengths of parties into consideration. Although India is a multi-party system the dominance of the Congress party renders the opposition of other political parties almost as negligible as that existing in nominally one-party systems. Conversely, a nominally one-party system may, for the sake of appearances, tolerate token opposition from other small parties.

A key determinant of a party system is reckoned to be the electoral system: proportional representation being associated with multi-party systems and the simple majority system of election with two-party systems. However, both this simple dichotomy and the argument that proportional representation leads to political instability can be over-stated. The method of election may itself be a product of perceptions that the electorate is either sufficiently consensual in its outlook to be able to accept the 'rough and ready' justice of the simple majority system or sufficiently riven by cleavages to justify the more sensitive and varied methods of proportional representation. The contrasting outcomes of similar electoral systems give the lie, however, to the notion that the method of election is the only determinant of party systems, or always the most important.

When we consider the Spanish party system, we have to acknowledge that the system is in its early stages of evolution: thus any definitive judgements are premature. If, for example, one considers the development of either the Irish or West German party systems in the first fifteen years of their existence, one can see the dangers of giving an early verdict. Early observers of the embryonic Spanish party system *circa* 1982 (Maravall 1982; Linz 1980) thought that they saw developing what Sartori (1978) had referred to as 'polarized pluralism', a system that is dominated by two pairs or sets of parties between which power can theoretically and, in practice, alternate. Since 1982, the convincing victories of the PSOE render even this provisional judgement somewhat dated. Although the PSOE percentage of the vote fell between 1982 and 1986, the gap between the PSOE and the Alianza Popular (Coalición Popular in 1986) was wide enough after both elections to raise doubts as to whether the Alianza constitutes a polar alternative to the PSOE. While the Alianza (and its later equivalent, the Coalición) and the PSOE together polled 70 per cent of the vote in both elections, there was a gap between the PSOE and its right-wing rival of 21 per cent in 1982, and 18 per cent in 1986. Thus, while the two parties have a control over the voters' loyalties rivalling that exercised by the two major parties in West Germany, the imbalance between the two parties and the inherent fissures within the Coalición Popular, make the term 'bipolar' inaccurate. It may be more accurate to describe the system as 'multi-party' with one dominant party in government, and one party dominant in opposition (Pollack and Hunter 1987: 371), but even that may exaggerate the strength of the opposition. In the late 1980s the system is looking more like a 'predominant party system' in the sense that any foreseeable opposition to the PSOE will require coalitions to be formed. The position of the PSOE is thus similar to, but currently stronger than, that of Fianna Fáil in the Republic of Ireland. This is true despite the slump in the PSOE's popularity since 1987 and the tarnished charisma of Gonzalez.

It is possible that the PSOE will succeed in maintaining its predominance, at least as long as the expectation of an alteration is not yet feasible. This means that the party system is not yet structured in a stable and lasting manner but remains open to the appearance of new actors on the scene. (Caciagli 1984: 96)

These 'new actors' are as likely to emanate from the centre of the political spectrum as from the right since it was the centre that saw something of a revival in its fortunes in the 1986 election. In the meantime, however, the pledge of Sr Gonzalez to extend the appeal of his party beyond the traditional confines of a 'workers' socialist' party has been honoured: the PSOE has become a 'catch-all' party by drawing electoral support from virtually all regions of the country, and across the whole range of social classes. The PSOE had benefited in 1982 from the 'flight' of voters from both the centrist UCD and the more extreme left PCE (Gunther 1985). The all-embracing latitude of PSOE policies in the 1980s has made the party a very 'broad church'.

Chapter three
The regions: a resumption of change

Introduction

One of the most remarkable achievements of the Spanish state since 1977 has been the accommodation of demands for regional autonomy. These demands did not emerge out of thin air but were a resumption of a process that had been abruptly aborted on the outbreak of the civil war in 1936 and suppressed during the long dictatorship of General Franco. However, the process of regionalization in the Spanish political system, in the period since 1977, has gone much further than anything that was envisaged in 1936. Nor has the process been unique to Spain: during the 1970s, many West European states have experienced demands for either autonomy or independence from regions within their boundaries. From Scotland in the north to Sardinia in the south, new political parties have challenged the authority of the central government as well as the redistributive assumptions on which the modern democratic welfare state is based. Although the pressures for autonomy within Spain are characterized by many features that are peculiar to the Spanish context, it is instructive to consider, as a preliminary to any discussion of the Spanish case, the broader West European experience of regional assertiveness.

Demands for regional autonomy have been a feature of many advanced West European states in the post-war period. These demands, often expressed in the language of raised ethnic consciousness, have constituted a species of 'proto-nationalism' exhibiting many features reminiscent of the great nation-building episodes in the nineteenth century. They have been firmly rooted in political and economic grievances and are symptomatic of the modern state's inability to satisfy adequately the increasing demands made on it. When the state becomes over-extended, the well-organized groups with ready access to central decision-making institutions are most likely to cream off the best of the scarce resources that are available. Those who suffer are the less well-organized minorities and peripheral regions. As the central organs of the state fail to respond to the rising expectations being generated by highly mobilized electorates, the regions that feel most remote from central decision-making agitate for more control over their own affairs. Political grievances are given added impetus by perceptions of economic deprivation or the experience of exploitation. The discovery of North Sea oil fuelled a Scottish nationalism that was partly based on perceptions that a valuable resource on Scotland's doorstep was being 'siphoned away' for England's benefit. Likewise, in Corsica and Brittany, investment that came into the region was all too often likely to leave again in the form of profits. In these regions, as elsewhere, there was a growing awareness that the local economy was as dependent as that of any colony.

Peripherality does not always connote economic backwardness. An economically advanced region on the geographic periphery of a large nation-state may feel as aggrieved as a less developed region. Here, the sense of grievance arises from a sense of being exploited by the central government for the purpose of subsidizing poorer regions.

Writers have offered various explanations for the rise of what is sometimes called sub-state nationalism. One of the best known is 'internal colonialism' (Hechter 1974) where it is argued that poorer regions are virtually 'colonized' by more advanced regions within the same state; the exploitation of the former is both a result and a condition of the latter's economic advance. Another explanation links the movement for regional autonomy to uneven economic development which, if exacerbated by ethnic cleavages coinciding with lines of economic deprivation, leads to political activism and even violence. A third theory, relevant to the Basque country, associates periods of rapid industrialization with a developing ethnic consciousness that may be sharpened by any large-scale influx of immigrants seeking work. In such a scenario, economic pressures may be coupled to cultural retrenchment as individuals feeling alienated by seismic shifts of the social landscape cling more tenaciously to familiar cultural roots.

> Small wonder then if a Welshman, Basque or Breton, the distinctiveness of whose region or culture may be diminished but is far from dead, should grasp at the idea of regional autonomy as the last chance of giving his life individual meaning. (Mayo 1974: 2)

When we turn to consider the pressures for regional autonomy in Spain it is helpful to keep these theoretical insights in mind.

Regionalism in Spain

The second article of the Spanish Constitution says:

> The Constitution is based on the indissoluble unity of the Spanish Nation, the common and indivisible fatherland – Patria – of all Spaniards, and recognizes and guarantees the right to self-government of the nationalities and regions of which it is composed and solidarity among them all.

The inclusion of the word 'nationalities' was obviously both controversial and historic in its implications. On the one hand, it clearly recognized the aspirations of communities like the Basques and Catalans to achieve a degree of autonomy undreamt of during the Franco period; and it implicitly called into question the integrity of the 'Spanish nation' itself. On the other hand, the word 'nationality' denoted people rather than political institutions, and it excluded the concept of a 'state': thus the ardent centralist could be reassured that recognition could be given to nationality while denying the right of citizenship in a separate state. Nevertheless, the introduction of the word 'nationality' sparked off a major debate in Spain throughout 1978, and its inclusion must be reckoned an act of considerable political courage. At the time, public opinion was deeply divided on the issue: while 75 per cent of respondents in one poll said they were in favour of giving 'autonomy' to 'regions and nationalities', another poll saw 40 per cent saying they were opposed to the word 'nationalities' appearing in the Constitution, 33 per cent in favour and 25 per cent undecided (Arbos 1985). To appreciate the extent and variety of progress made in Spain towards implementing regional autonomy, we now turn to a discussion of three contrasting cases: Galicia, Catalonia and the Basque country.

Galicia

Galicia is a region of north-western Spain covering an area of 29,153 square kilometres. Geographically, it is cut off from the rest of Spain by high mountains to the east, and the Portuguese border to the south. The topography is hilly although the average elevation above sea level ranges from 200 to 600 metres. The climate is wet: more than 40 inches of rain fall annually, and the many rivers draining into the Atlantic provide a rich source of hydroelectricity, principally for the rest of Spain. The regional economy is dominated by agricultural occupations; the growing of potatoes and maize and the rearing of pigs being particularly important. The demographic profile of the region is somewhat unbalanced due to widespread emigration of younger people to other parts of Spain and to Latin America. Fish and timber provide other exports from the region: Vigo is Spain's leading fishing port. There is also some shipbuilding in Vigo and El Ferrol.

The first stirrings of Galician nationalism were not really apparent until the nineteenth century because of the region's economic marginality. Towards the end of the century, a handful of intellectuals began to cultivate an interest in the region's history and culture. As early as 1843, Faraldo had called for Galician independence but he was premature: the region's history was definitively inscribed by Murguia in the early years of the twentieth century in a work called *Historia de Galicia.* Newspapers like *El Clamor de Galicia* and *El Recreo de Galicia* had already awakened a spirit of self-determination. A book entitled *El Regionalismo* appeared in 1889, formulating the idea of Galician autonomy in overtly political terms for the first time. The same writer, Branas, was also responsible for editing an autonomist newspaper *Patria Gallega* at about the same time. As is often the case with ethnic diaspora, the autonomist ideas found favour with emigrant groups: Galician nationalism flourished in Havana, Cuba, amongst other cities in the New World.

At the turn of the century a number of organizations sprang up in Galicia, each dedicated to the stimulation of nationalist feeling. In 1897 Liga Galega was founded; in 1907 Solidaridade Galega was formed with a mainly rural membership base; two other organizations – Aición Galega (1911) and Irmandade da Fala (1916) – followed shortly afterwards. The nationalist movement found its basic text in *Teoria do Nacionalismo Galego* (1920) published by Vicente Risco, the editor of a nationalist review entitled *Nos.* In 1929, ORGA (Organización Republicana Galega Autónoma) produced the leader Quiroga who represented Galicia in the Pact of San Sebastian (1930) where the future recognition of Galician identity was formally agreed. In 1931, the Partido Galeguista (PG) was founded which openly planned an autonomy statute for the region. In 1936 a split occurred within the party between a left and right wing, the left wing eventually leading the party under Castelao to victory in the polls of 1936 where autonomy was accepted by 993,351 votes to 6,161.

The outbreak of the civil war, only three days after the presentation of the Statute to the Cortes, stopped the autonomy process dead in its tracks. Many Galician nationalists found themselves exiled to South America which became a haven for militant autonomists. Buenos Aires, for example, became a well-known centre for Galician nationalists in exile.

In Galicia itself, repression under Franco virtually reduced any overt signs of regional sentiment to insignificance. The regime waged an unrelenting campaign against Galician culture and the Galician language. Posters appeared admonishing the people: 'Don't be a country bumpkin, speak Spanish!' At the same time, all the worst features of the backward rural economy were left untouched: lopsided land distribution, an oppressed peasantry, absentee landlords and steady emigration.

Until 1950, there was some co-operation between the PCE and the PG but this soon crumbled under the wider pressures of the Cold War at the national level. The PG dissolved itself and its members devoted themselves to cultural activities. In the 1960s, the Consello da Mocedade (the Council of Youth) spawned two movements with strong separatist tendencies: the Unión do Povo Galego (UPG) with strong socialist and revolutionary ideals, and the Partido Socialista Galego of a more moderate and social democratic inclination. The UPG, having absorbed the left wing of the Consello da Mocedade, former PG members, and younger elements from the Communist Party (PCE), made its goal the self-determination of the Galician people and their eventual independence from the Spanish state. The party denounced the 'colonial exploitation' that the Galician people had allegedly suffered at the hands of the Spanish 'oligarchy' and its 'imperialist state'. Allied to, and in sympathy with, the Basque separatist group ETA, the UPG intended to organize an 'armed struggle' but these plans were nipped in the bud by police action in 1975 which threw the would-be guerrillas into considerable disarray.

The regionalization of Galician politics was reflected in the increasing insertion of the letter 'G' into the names of regional parties. The PCE in Galicia became the PCG (Partido Comunista Gallego) and in 1975 a Partido Galego Socialdemocrata (PGSD) was created, with the Maoist Movemento Comunista Gallego (MCG) also joining the campaign for regional self-determination. Divisions within and among the parties arguing for autonomy or independence resulted in an electoral victory for the right in the 1977 elections: the UCD gained twenty seats, the Alianza Popular four. On the left, only the PSOE won any seats in the Cortes.

A referendum on the question of autonomy was held in Galicia in December 1980. While only 26 per cent of the electorate participated, 71 per cent of those voting endorsed a regional autonomy statute advocated by most of the political parties. The original draft of the statute had been supported only by the UCD, but later amendment enabled the PSOE in particular to throw its weight behind the autonomy process. During the electoral campaign in the region, the UCD, PSOE, the Democratic Coalition, the Communist Party, the

Unified Communist Party, The Carlist Party and the Galician party urged a 'yes' vote. The statute was opposed by the (Marxist–Leninist) National Popular Bloc, the Union of the Galician people (UPG) and the more extreme right-wing and left-wing parties.

The most recent elections in Galicia took place in November 1985. As in the previous elections (in 1981) the Popular Alliance (AP), contesting the poll as the principal component in the Popular Coalition (CP) won the most votes but failed to gain an absolute majority in the 71-seat regional parliament. Seats were lost to the new centrist Galician Coalition (CG) which took eleven seats and to the PSOE's Galician branch (PSDG–PSOE). The Popular Coalition took 34 seats (40.4 per cent); the PSDG–PSOE took 22 seats (28.3 per cent); the CG took eleven seats (12.8 per cent); the PSG–EG (Galician Socialist Party–Galician Left) took three seats (5.6 per cent of the vote); and the BNG (Galician Nationalist Block) fell from three seats in 1981 to one in 1985 with just 3.2 per cent of the votes cast.

Like Basque and Catalan, the Galician language is the cultural badge of its region. Similar to Portuguese, it is only in the twentieth century that it has been fostered. Under the Franco regime its use became a form of defiant resistance against the monolingual and centralizing policies of the dictatorship. Even before the civil war, Galician had never been the language of the middle classes, and its relatively humble status (as compared with Catalan for example) led to it being put on only an equal footing with Castilian in the autonomy Statute of 1936. The implication that upwardly mobile groups in Galician society would learn and speak Castilian and that to speak the vernacular was to concede a parochial outlook has never really disappeared, and it is linked to the broader 'collective inferiority complex' specified by one writer (Diaz Lopez 1982) as being the hallmark of Galician nationalism. Nevertheless, the language made some progress in the 1960s when the Church admitted it to the liturgy, and the University of Santiago de Compostela began to nurture academic interest in regional culture. Regional political parties have made some headway in getting the language taken more seriously, but the widespread assumption that Castilian is the key to modernity militates against the language in a region that considers itself economically deprived.

The Galician economy has been almost as isolated from the rest of Spain as the language; and its main features are still subsistence farming on the minifundia, 91 per cent of which are under 20 hectares in size. In 1970, about half of Galicia's population was engaged in primary occupations, compared with about a quarter in the rest of Spain. Galicia is more densely populated (87 people per square kilometre) than the average for the rest of the country (67 per square kilometre), and much less urbanized. Only 15 per cent of Galicians live in towns or cities with a population above 100,000, the lowest proportion in Spain. Emigration has been a major consequence of economic underdevelopment: half a million people left the region between 1950 and 1973, leaving behind a distinctly top-heavy demographic profile (in rural areas two-thirds of the population are over 55). In common with other similarly backward regions in Western Europe, there is a distinct cleavage between the cities where economic activity is focused on the outside world and virtually ignores the hinterland, and the rural areas that are preoccupied with their own survival and have little contact with their own urban areas. There is the same circularity of economic forces that tends to emphasize the region's disadvantage: labour drifts away to seek work elsewhere, leaving behind the old and the young; banks invest in more profitable regions; and the area's natural resources are 'plundered' by the more advanced sectors of the economy. Galicia, for example, generates a quarter of Spain's hydroelectricity, but some areas of Galicia have no electricity at all. Regional politics are based therefore on this sense of exploitation by a process of 'internal colonialism' familiar in other parts of the West European periphery. Apparently beneficial steps, such as motorway construction or the advent of nuclear power, are resisted as being of no long-term benefit to Galicia itself.

Catalonia

Catalonia is a region in north-eastern Spain covering an area of 31,929 square kilometres. It consists of the provinces of Gerona, Lerida, Barcelona, and Tarragona. The region is cut off from France by the Pyrenees, from Aragon by the Ebro basin, and from Valencia in the south by low ranges of coastal hills. These same hills extend northwards to divide the region into two main zones: one the industrial littoral with busy cities like Barcelona; and an inland zone dominated by smaller towns and a mainly agricultural economy. The climate is principally a Mediterranean one, with rainfall amounts varying from about 11 inches per annum in the Ebro basin to more than 35 inches in the foothills of the Pyrenees. The coastal plain is heavily populated, and most of the region's inhabitants live here. One-third of the land is under cultivation although the traditional crops of grapes and olives are being replaced by fruit and vegetables in response to demand from shifting patterns of consumption in the EEC. Although likely to remain an important part of the Catalonian economy, agriculture accounts for only 10 per cent of its gross domestic product, and 10 per cent of its workforce. The bulk of the economy is taken up by the industrial and service sectors. The traditional textile industry is now giving way to metal-working, chemical industries and petroleum refineries, all focused on Barcelona and its environs. The city is also the site of a major car factory.

Catalonia's history as a region with its own political institutions dates back to 1289 when the establishment of the Generalitat de Catalunya defined the traditional Catalonian liberties and privileges as a bastion against the centralizing encroachments of the Spanish Crown. Catalonian political identity was eclipsed after 1410 when the male line of the counts of Barcelona became extinct. A sustained but ultimately unsuccessful attempt to reassert Catalonian autonomy took the form of a rebellion between 1462 and 1472, but after the unification of Spain in 1469 Catalonia became subsumed in the wider kingdom. In the middle of the seventeenth century, Catalonia managed to assert its independence from the Spanish monarchy and only rejoined the Hapsburg state after its autonomy had been guaranteed. However, in 1716, a royal decree entitled Decreto de Nueva Planta formally abolished Catalonian autonomy.

Any discussion of Catalonian culture must take into account two preliminary caveats: the area affected by the culture extends beyond Catalonia itself to, among other places, the Balearics and Valencia; and the culture is not simply a middle-class phenomenon even if the middle class may seem to have appropriated it. The victory of Philip V in 1714 ended Catalonian resistance to the centralizing monarchy, and Catalonia's culture virtually hibernated until the nineteenth century. The language was suppressed, the local institutions abolished, the culture itself rendered marginal at best. In the early nineteenth century, there was something of a cultural revival in parallel with what was happening in other parts of Western Europe. This awakening took two distinct forms: in the countryside, there was support for a complete restoration of the *fueros* removed in 1714, and a return to an absolutist form of rule. In the city, the movement was more progressive, democratic and federalist with an emphasis on local centres of power. During the century, literature and the study of Catalonian history bloomed. The latter pursuit revived a pride in Catalonia's traditional institutions and underlined their validity. The cultural revival was accompanied and indeed assisted by economic activity: the quickening pace of commercial activity spurred on the desire for greater political self-determination. From the 1870s onwards, publications in Catalan became more frequent: the first Catalan newspaper, *Diari Catala,* appeared before the end of the century, as did a book on Catalan culture entitled *Lo Catalanisme* (1886).

In the twentieth century, more radical groups appeared. Accio Catalana was started in 1922 but the budding nationalist movement was becalmed again during the dictatorship of Primo de Rivera (1923–30). The policies of the dictator could not completely quench the desire of the Catalans for a recognition of their own cultural identity. The dictator banned Catalan in schools, and even tried to outlaw the *sardana,* the Catalan regional dance. In 1932, political autonomy was achieved under the restored Generalitat. Under the Statute of Autonomy, Catalonia was given control over almost all its own affairs except those pertaining to its external relations.

In the civil war, Catalonia sided with the Republic but was eventually overwhelmed by Franco's forces. The dictator cancelled the Autonomy Statute, and instigated a long campaign of repression against the economy, politics and culture of the region. The long repression served only to reinforce the desire of the Catalans to regain their autonomy. Within the region, resistance against the central government was mounted by Communists and Socialists, as well as groups in the centre. After 1977, it was clear that although almost all parties in Catalonia were agreed on the need for autonomy, there would be a fierce struggle between them for control of the transitional process. In the first elections in 1977, the left-wing parties carried the day, and the appointment of Tarradellas (the former premier of Republican Catalonia) later the same year placed the central government's seal of approval on the autonomy process. In 1979, the region voted on a new Autonomy Statute in a referendum that achieved 89 per cent support (although 40 per cent abstention) and paved the way for the first elections to the restored Generalitat in 1980. In these elections, Pujol's Convergencia i Unio (CiU), a strongly nationalist party, took 43 of the 135 seats with the Catalan Socialist Party (PSC) coming second with 33 seats. In a coalition with the UCD and Esquerra, Pujol formed the first government in Catalonia since the civil war.

The existence of a separate Catalan government since 1980, with its own regional institutions, has helped the long-suppressed sense of Catalan national identity to flourish. In a poll among young people in Barcelona in 1984, 27 per cent said they felt 'only Catalan' and a further 16 per cent felt more 'Catalan than Spanish'. Nineteen per cent said they would like to see an independent Catalan state (Melich, Viros and Treserra 1985). Other research has shown that the sense of Catalan nationalism is strongest among those who have one or both parents born in Catalonia, but even those who have moved to Catalonia recently identify strongly with the region and call themselves Catalans by virtue of 'living and working here', an attitude that is carefully cultivated by political parties anxious to garner the immigrant vote. Language is clearly a badge of Catalan identity: those who do not speak it find jobs difficult to get and the pressure to learn the language and become integrated into Catalan society is therefore almost irresistible.

Catalans refer to their region as a *país* (country) and a *nación* (nation) and base these assertions on past history, linguistic distinctiveness, and a feeling of 'being different' from the Castilian majority in Spain. Catalans have few problems with what is essentially a double identity: while a few feel exclusively Catalan or exclusively Spanish, most feel that both labels apply to them although in differing degrees. There is little awareness of any conflict between the two identities: one is seen as a subdivision of the other in the same way that Scots see no contradiction in also calling themselves British. The appeal of Catalan nationalism crosses class lines although the hurdle of learning the Catalan language means necessarily that many immigrants from other parts of Spain (for example, Andalucía) are in less well-paid jobs or jobs that require less training. However, on a left–right axis Catalan nationalism tends to be supported more strongly on the left, while right-wing voters and parties are perceived as being more sympathetic to centralization and limitations on regional independence. For this reason, political parties with a regional base, whether of the centre or the left, do better than those who have no regional affiliations. Thus the PSOE and the PSC present a common list at elections so as to maximize the appeal of both among *españolistas* and Catalans. Likewise, while the PCE is shunned in Catalonia as a centralizing party, the Catalan equivalent, the PSUC, is accepted as having respectable autonomist credentials.

The most recent regional elections in Catalonia took place in April 1984. In these, the main nationalist party, the Convergence and Union (CiU), won an absolute majority with 72 seats in the 135-member parliament and 46.6 per cent of the vote. The main loser was the Unified Socialist Party of Catalonia (PSUC) which won only six seats compared with 25 in the 1980 elections. A total of 64.4 per cent of the Catalan electorate went to the polls. Sr Pujol was re-elected prime minister by 87 votes to 44. His re-election was a personal triumph as well as a political one, as he had been charged shortly after the election result with embezzlement and falsification of documents relating to deposits in the Bank of Catalonia; Sr Pujol had himself founded the bank in 1958, but had resigned in 1982 in order to devote himself to politics. Responding to accusations that the charges had been engineered by the Madrid government as revenge for its trouncing in the provincial elections, Sr Gonzalez said that the public

49

prosecutor acted quite independently of government and, indeed, that the central government had rescued the Bank of Catalonia in 1982 at the cost of 270,000 million pesetas.

Violence has rarely been used by Catalonian separatists, but in October 1986 an organization called Terra Lluire (Free Land) claimed responsibility for two bomb explosions in Barcelona. These attacks were apparently a protest against the city's success in winning the nomination as the location for the Olympic Games in 1992. The group feared that such an event would smother Catalonian identity under a blanket of international media attention. As has happened in the Basque country, an anti-separatist terrorist group has emerged in Catalonia called Milicia Catalana and claimed responsibility for bombing two well-known bookshops in the city and leaving behind leaflets declaring, amongst other things, 'Long live brotherhood among the peoples of Spain! Long live the unity of the country!' In August 1986, the same group started a major forest fire near the ninth-century monastery of Montserrat, a symbolic shrine of Catalonian nationalism and a popular tourist attraction.

The Basque country

The Basque country covers an area of about 20,000 square kilometres and encompasses four provinces in northern Spain; Alava, Navarra, Guipuzcoa, and Vizcaya, as well as three provinces in south-western France. The bulk of the Basque territory (85 per cent) lies, and most of its inhabitants (90 per cent) live, on the Spanish side of the border. The population of the Spanish Basque country is about 2.3 million, of whom only 65 per cent are native Basques. The effect of an international border running through the region has had mixed effects on Basque regional identity. On the one hand it has clearly weakened Basque collective identity by creating two very different relationships with the respective central governments (Lancaster 1987), but on the other hand the border has, until recently, provided a refuge from which militant Basques could sustain more effectively their campaign in Spain.

The Basque region is ethnically distinct and geographically cut off by rugged mountains from the rest of Spain. This impervious ethnicity, only penetrated by the influx of outsiders drawn by economic opportunities, is reflected in an idiosyncratic language that has no known connection with any other European tongue, and whose origins are still almost completely obscure. Language is clearly the defining cultural variable of the region despite the fact that fewer than half of native-born Basques actually speak it. Economically, the

Basque country is, like Catalonia, one of the more developed parts of Spain although the extent of industrialization has been very uneven with Navarre still largely dependent upon agriculture, and the area around Bilbao displaying all the worst characteristics of 'smokestack industries'. Industrial development in the region has created a demand for labour, and immigration into the Basque country from other parts of Spain has been one ingredient in the upsurge of Basque nationalism, the influx of outsiders inevitably producing something of a cultural 'siege mentality' among the Basques themselves.

Politically, the region has had a long but rarely unchallenged record of separate administration. A form of autonomy, under jealously guarded *fueros* or local statutes, each province having its own, dates back to the seventh century. An uneasy relationship whereby the Basques maintained a separate identity under the umbrella of allegiance to Madrid suited both sides until the nineteenth century. From then onwards, the *fueros* were slowly eroded so that by the end of the century centralizing rule from Castile had virtually dismantled them, although the respective tax liabilities of the provinces and the central government remained a subject for negotiation with Madrid until the Spanish Civil War (1936-9). The twin pressures of industrialization and political centralization stimulated a revival of Basque nationalism.

The revival cannot be attributed to a single factor, but both the sparks that lit the fire as well as the fuel that kept it alight, appear to have been the challenges posed to traditional Basque society and its economy by the inroads of new industry and the self-interest of entrepreneurs who had roots outside the region. In this context, the abolition of the *fueros* in 1876 and, in particular, the removal of the customs posts on the Ebro, and with them an important symbol and component of economic autonomy, marked a watershed in relations between the Basques and Madrid. In the early years of the twentieth century the Basque country went through the same struggles for industrial democracy as characterized other parts of Western Europe: the right to strike, conceded in 1909, followed the formation of the first trade union, the Unión General de Trabajadores (UGT) in 1882. None the less, many Basques saw these issues as subsidiary to that of national autonomy, believing that it was within the structures of a Basque state that other goals could be best achieved.

The wave of nationalism brought forth its first nationalist leader in the person of Sabino de Arana, born in 1865 and destined to found the Basque nationalist party, Partido Nacional Vasco (PNV) in 1895. Arana gave shape to the cause of Basque nationalism by baptizing the new state Euskadi, designing its flag, and working to encourage the dissemination of the Basque language. Arana laid the foundations of Basque nationalist ideology which, among other things, comprised a dedication to the Catholic faith, the espousal of non-violent methods to achieve political goals, the belief that all Basques should be united across the Pyrenees, and the assertion that language should be the defining characteristic of the Basque race. With few modifications, and with a flexible view on the appropriate political structures to underpin these goals, these principles have remained the core of PNV orthodoxy right up to the present time.

It is apparent from what has been said that the Basque language, Euskera, is a central focus for Basque nationalism. Under the pressures of industrialization and immigration it had become very much a rural language by the end of the nineteenth century. Lacking vocabulary to convey new inventions and concepts, it was forced to absorb neologisms. From 1936 onwards, under the dictatorship of General Franco, the language was banned in public, its teaching forbidden, and books in Basque were burned. This assault on the principal defining feature of Basque culture was a deliberate attempt by the dictatorship to stamp out a regionalism that was perceived as a threat to the organic unity of the State whose integrity was deemed a precondition of its effectiveness. However, even before Franco died in 1975, Euskera was reasserting itself. In 1955, a Chair of Basque Studies was established at the University of Salamanca; and in 1975 the 'co-official' status of Basque as a language was formally recognized. Today, the language, although no longer officially discouraged, is still used only by a minority and more commonly among the old than the young: the years of repression have taken their toll. Among the Basque provinces, the usage of the language is extremely variable: only one per cent of the population speak it in Alava, while just over 40 per cent do so in Guipuzcoa.

Unlike either Catalonia or Galicia, the Basque country has seen its nationalist aspirations translated into political violence. Euskadi ta Askatasuna (ETA) began as a simple nationalist movement with Basque independence as its sole objective. It was founded by a group within the PNV in the early 1950s and was a reaction to the stagnation and sense of futility experienced by younger nationalists within an established party, and against an atmosphere of repression under Franco. At its inception, ETA did not advocate violence as a method of achieving political change, but was forced onto this road by the tactics of the Franco regime and its gratuitous physical suppression of any visible symbol of Basque national identity. At the organization's congress in 1966–7 a commitment to the 'armed struggle' was made.

The first fatalities occurred in 1968, and during the next few years, hundreds of Basques were imprisoned without trial. In December 1970, six were given a military trial and sentenced to death (the sentences being subsequently commuted to thirty years in prison). The Burgos Trial became a *cause célèbre* and attracted worldwide attention to both the character of the Franco regime and the cause of Basque nationalism. The trial also had the unintended effect of stimulating recruitment to the ranks of ETA: when leaders disappeared into prison, there were always volunteers to take their place.

By 1974, a more extreme element within ETA broke away and formed ETA–M (ETA–militar) leaving ETA–PM (politico-militar) as the custodians of the 'twin-track' approach: the bomb and the ballot paper in a varying mix. From then on the initiative lay with the ETA–M faction: it carried out the worst atrocities in the 1970s, the murder of the prime minister Admiral Carrero Blanco in 1973, the killing of 13 people at the Café Rolando in Madrid the following year, and frequent assassinations of Guardia Civil officers in the 1980s.

ETA represents what might be termed the 'cutting edge' of nationalist sentiment in the Basque country. Besides the PNV there are two other parties that advocate Basque autonomy/independence, Euskadiko Eskerra (EE) and Herri Batasuna (HB) both of which were founded in the 1970s and both advocating more extreme tactics than the PNV. Although nationalist parties muster between them over half the regional vote, there are deep divisions over tactics between the three parties.

The PNV sees itself as the 'responsible' party of Basque nationalism and tries to appeal to a broad section of the electorate: it has, for example, advocated a choice between Basque and Spanish as the language of instruction in schools. It avoids being easily classified as a party of the right or the left, and while advocating the constitutional road towards greater independence, is careful in its public statements on the subject of ETA, preferring to characterize them as 'misguided' rather than 'criminal'. HB is the most extreme of the three parties, and stands for elections on an abstentionist basis. It has been associated with the more militant of the two ETA factions (ETA–M) but its electoral popularity actually rose slightly in the 1986 elections while that of the PNV declined. EE participates in political institutions arguing that the system is best changed from within. Like HB, it advocates the teaching of Basque in schools, the withdrawal of Spanish troops from Basque soil and various measures against capitalism. In the 1986 general election the PNV won six seats, the HB five seats, and EE two seats. These results indicated a significant radicalization of Basque politics with moderate nationalism losing out to the more extreme varieties (Robinson 1987).

The extent to which members of groups like ETA live apart from the society they inhabit is a topic that has attracted a certain amount of academic attention. In the case of the Provisional IRA, for example, all the evidence (Burton 1978; Heskin 1980) points towards activists being very representative of the people they live among. Similar observations have been made about members of ETA: the *etarras*. In an analysis of a group of *etarras* in 1979–80, Clark (Merkl 1986) found them to be typical young members of small-town Basque society, not alienated from their communities, sometimes self-employed (as carpenters, builders, and so on) or sometimes in middle-class occupations such as teaching or banking. *Etarras* were more likely to have Basque parentage than most inhabitants of the Basque country, but there was no evidence that they suffered specific grievances as individuals, simply the generalized grievances of Basque society. Most *etarras* were from Basque-speaking areas, and thus unusually conscious of the ethnic identity in a society where Basque is no longer spoken by the majority of people. The cultural shock of being sent to schools where Spanish was the only language allowed, and linguistic clumsiness construed as academic backwardness, reinforced a sense of alienation in many *etarras* at an early age.

Under Franco, harassment by the police further emphasized this feeling of alienation: playing Basque musical instruments, singing Basque songs, or wearing the Basque national colours were sufficient reasons to attract the unwelcome attentions of the Guardia Civil. Persecution by the police has tended to swell the ranks of ETA. Almost all *etarras* live with their families, and see their time in ETA as a short but stressful part-time occupation that does not interfere with their everyday gainful employment. Clark reckons that ETA activists operate in their own neighbourhoods and that the peculiarly Basque social unit, the *cuadrilla* (a gang of four or five male comrades), makes the perfect basis for an *etarra* cell (Merkl 1986).

The right of the Basque people to determine their own fate lies at the heart of ETA ideology, and provides the theoretical underpinning for the campaign of violence. Although the democratization of the Spanish state changes the context within which the struggle must be fought, the need for the struggle itself has not diminished. The new democratic monarchy is perceived as being a sham democracy that has not really reformed the system, nor dislodged the 'real powers' (*poderes facticos*) such as the Army, the Church and the banks. The Basques are still denied their independence, and ETA can point to the undeniable fact that the Spanish Constitution was rejected by 63 per cent of the voters in the Basque country and thus has little claim to legitimacy in the region. ETA rejects the view that its own socialist tendencies should prevent it from attacking an avowedly socialist government, because PSOE is deemed to have broken almost all its major electoral promises. ETA justifies its armed struggle in terms familiar to other similar groups in Western Europe: the need to 'raise consciousness' among the Basque people, the duty to 'protect' the people against the repressive apparatus of central government, and the necessity of confronting the government in the only language it understands. The conditions under which ETA would consider a ceasefire include an amnesty for all ETA prisoners, the legalization of all political parties, the withdrawal of Spanish security forces from the Basque country, and the passing of an authentic autonomy statute with Euskera as the official language (*Cambio 16*, 12 May 1986).

The ETA campaign of violence is carefully orchestrated to create conditions in which counter-measures by the state's security forces are likely to provoke a certain degree of revulsion on the part of the region's population. Some attacks have a clear symbolic intent: a well-known figure is assassinated because of what he represents. One such attack was the murder of General Lago Roman in November 1982 in Madrid. The timing was a crucial factor in the planning of the whole episode: the first PSOE government was due to take office a few days later, and already the temptation for the Army to pre-empt this event was strong. The Pope was visiting Spain and thus the media coverage of the assassination was likely to be extensive. Lago Roman was no ordinary general: he was the commander of the Brunete division, the most powerful in the Spanish Army, and one with special responsibility for protecting the nation's capital. It was from Brunete, moreover, that an abortive coup had been launched in 1981, and the name 'Brunete' was itself an echo of a famous victory in the Civil War achieved by Francoist forces against the Republicans. With such a target, and such a sensitive moment in Spain's transition to democracy, ETA had a good chance of provoking a security 'backlash' in the Basque country itself which might result in a shift of moderate Basque opinion towards ETA.

Two-thirds of all of ETA's victims are members of the security forces (Merkl 1986) and most of these are members of the Guardia Civil. It has been estimated that between 1968 and 1980 about 240 people have died as a result of ETA actions, making the fatality rates lower than those of Northern Ireland or Beirut. Since 1980, the annual fatality rate from ETA operations has fallen off somewhat, due partly to security measures taken by the Government, and partly to growing support for non-violent means of achieving autonomy in the region. The ETA campaign has become more selective, and it has extended its operations outside the Basque country. An independent unit appeared to be operating in Madrid in the early and mid-1980s with some dramatic atrocities attributable to its members. The political fall-out from killing members of the police or Army in the national capital are proportionately greater than in the Basque country itself, just as the IRA makes a greater political–psychological impact on the British mainland.

The Spanish government has adopted a variety of strategies for containing violence in the Basque country. First, it has pushed ahead with autonomy for the region in the hope of undercutting support for ETA. Second, it has taken steps to make the security forces more effective in the region. Third, it has increased co-operation with France in the hope of eliminating French territory as a base and refuge for ETA activists.

As we have seen, a section of the Spanish Constitution was devoted to the issue of granting autonomy to the regions. The Basque country was one of the first regions, the other being Catalonia, to receive a measure of regional autonomy by 1980. In its aims to have some measure of economic control returned to the region, and to re-establish a Basque police force, the PNV was undoubtedly aided by the continuing violence of ETA which went a long way towards softening up a central government whose approach otherwise to the whole question might have been more dilatory. The new police force started traffic duties in January 1981 while the national Guardia Civil remained responsible for security. The new Basque police force consisted of 500 at the outset but had grown to 5,000 by 1986. The economic agreements whereby the Basque government would again have the right to levy taxes came into effect at about the same time. The tax rates are the same as in the rest of Spain but only about one-third (the exact amount being fixed at five-yearly intervals) is handed over to the central government. The process of political autonomy in the Basque country has been plagued by tensions both within the ruling PNV, and between the regional government and the central government in Madrid. Following the Basque regional elections in 1984, the president of the Basque government, Sr Garaicoetxca, tried, despite pressure from within his own party, to persist with his policy of improving relations with the central government in Madrid with whom there had been a fair amount of dissension over the interpretation of the autonomy statute. In the autumn of 1984, the Basque president was called on, by a member of the opposition Coalición Popular, to explain the view of a PNV member that the party's goal was 'the formation of an integrated Basque state by its seven historic regions' (i.e. on both sides of the Pyrenees). Sr Garaicoetxca's non-committal reply was that 'co-existence is possible in a pluri-national state where a level of self-government is respected'. This exchange was symptomatic of a deeper divergence of views within the PNV relating to the degree of autonomy being sought for the Basque country. This issue was related in turn to a variety of attitudes within the PNV as to what the correct policy towards the abstentionist Herri Batasuna party ought to be with its eleven unfilled seats in the regional parliament. That there was a serious dispute within the leadership of the PNV, over the whole question of relations with the Madrid government, became clear when a document was leaked in September of the same year.

Sr Garaicoetxca resigned in December 1984 after a vote of no confidence in him was passed by his party. The resignation came at the end of a long period of governmental paralysis, brought about partly by the fact that the PNV did not have a working majority in the regional parliament, due to the refusal of the PSE–PSOE (the socialists in the Basque country) to co-operate with the PNV, and partly by the virtual breakdown of relations with the Madrid government, in this case over the question of whether the ultimate authority for allocating the regional budget lay with the regional government or with the region's constituent provinces, the *diputaciones forales*.

In January 1985, the Basque parliament endorsed Sr Ardanza as Garaicoetxca's successor. The new regional president lost no time in setting about the task of establishing a pact with the socialists in the Basque parliament so that a working majority could push ahead with economic reforms, a bi-partisan approach to ETA's violence, and a speedier transfer of powers to regional institutions.

The divergence of views within the PNV was widened by the party's losses in the 1986 general election. By the time of the next regional elections (in November 1986) the split in the PNV had become irrevocable and the dissidents left to form a new party, the Eusko Alkastasuna (EA) under Sr Ibarrondo. The PNV saw its seats in the regional parliament reduced from 32 to 17 but the loss was almost exactly mirrored by the newly-formed EA winning 14 seats. The new regional government, under Sr Ardanza was not formed until February 1987 but its solidity as a coalition between the PNV and the socialists was underlined by the post of vice-president being held by Sr Jauregui, a socialist, and the cabinet posts being distributed equally between the two parties.

On the security front new anti-terrorist legislation came into effect in 1980 in the form of an organic law as provided for under Article 55 of the constitution. This defined the circumstances governing the extension of preventive detention beyond 72 hours, the right to search homes without a warrant, and the interception of mail and telephone conversations. The new legislation, passed by parliament with an overwhelming majority, laid down that these rights could be suspended in relation to persons suspected of terrorist acts or complicity in defence of such acts. Preventive detention could be extended to ten days and postal observation or telephone tapping could be carried out for three months by order of a magistrate or in an emergency on the direct orders of the director of state security or the interior minister. Anti-terrorist legislation became part of the permanent laws of the state whereas hitherto, since 1978, such laws had been 'decree laws' subject to annual renewal. In the spring of 1981, in the wake of more serious incidents in the Basque country, the Government passed more anti-terrorist legislation through the Cortes. The crime of 'rebellion' was now defined as, amongst other things, obstructing parliament, impeding elections, inciting the Army against the Constitution, or depriving a member of the Government of his liberty. Various kinds of 'emergency' were defined in another law: a state of 'exception' could be declared by the Cortes for 30 days in the event of 'a grave alteration in the normal functioning of the democratic institutions', and this allowed the authorities to detain people for up to ten days, ban meetings, and suspend publications temporarily. A state of 'siege' could be declared by the Cortes in the event of an 'insurrection or act of force against the sovereignty or independence of Spain, its territorial integrity or its constitutional order', and in this case constitutional rights could be temporarily suspended.

In May 1983, following more violence in the Basque country, the interior minister announced the implementation of 'Operation ZEN' (Zona Especial del Norte) – a new security initiative – to provide better protection for civilians going about their daily business, especially banks, which had recently been coming under attack from ETA. Guardia Civil members were to be given special training, and special rates of remuneration, for their service in the Basque country. At the end of 1983, new laws were introduced that allowed judges to ban publications or political associations that supported terrorism; and detention without trial for up to two and a half years could be ordered. Sentences for terrorist offences were increased, while the bait of reduced sentences or quashed convictions was offered to suspects who turned informer.

The year 1984 marked the inauguration of a new tactic on the part of the Government. An amnesty, or 'social reintegration' as the policy was called, was offered to individual ETA members who agreed in writing to renounce terrorism. This offer was extended to ETA members in Spain and those abroad. In April, forty-three prisoners made a joint application for 'social reintegration' and news came of ETA members in exile in Latin America and France seeking permission to return to Spain under the new arrangements. Some controversy was stirred up by the interior minister's remark that he was prepared to negotiate with ETA but this statement was later 'clarified' to rule out concessions to ETA as an organization, and simply to refer to the offers open to individuals in the organization who wanted to lay down their arms. The PNV called the gesture 'not very realistic' and ETA–M dismissed it as a 'purely laughable manoeuvre'.

In 1985, rumours of further contacts between ETA-M and the Government continued to surface. The Government would only admit to informal contacts, not formal negotiations. An apparent lull in 1986 seemed to suggest that the policy of reintegration was beginning to make inroads into ETA's operations. However, the breakaway 'Spain Commando' of ETA carried out an attack on a police bus in Madrid in July killing twelve members of the Guardia Civil. An increasing involvement by the Basque regional police in security duties looked likely in the autumn after a gun battle between members of an ETA kidnap gang and the Ertzanta (Basque police). 1986 also saw the publication of a report by a commission set up by the Basque government and chaired by a retired British diplomat, Sir Clive Rose. Interestingly, the report's recommendations went some way beyond what the British government would countenance for dealing with the IRA in Northern Ireland, and probably beyond what the Spanish government feels it can reasonably do at the moment. Among the principal recommendations were: that negotiations with ETA should never be ruled out; that ETA terrorist cases should be tried in the normal courts and not in the special terrorist court in Madrid; that some attempt should be made to give positive recognition of Basque national identity in the framework of the European Economic Community; that the Ertzanta should gradually assume all responsibility for security in the region; and that steps should be taken to stimulate the region's economy. The suggestion that there should be negotiations with ETA stirred up heated discussions in the political parties. Herri Batasuna (the political wing of ETA) welcomed the suggestion but the regional government was not willing to go much beyond informal contacts. The central government in Madrid was less ambivalent. Sr Gonzalez said after the report had been published, 'There have not been, and there will not be, negotiations with ETA'.

Besides presenting an internal security problem, the aspirations of ETA have an irredentist dimension in so far as the eventual goal of ETA is to unite the French and Spanish parts of the region. Even if this stage of the strategy is rather remote, the existence of a Basque population on the French side of the Pyrenees provides ETA activists with a base and a refuge from which to launch operations on the Spanish security forces. Since 1980, however, co-operation between France and Spain has improved with tangible results. The reluctance of the French government to extradite Basque suspects to Spain stemmed partly from a residual distrust of Spanish justice inherited from the Franco period; partly from pride in the tradition of France itself as a *terre d'asile* – a haven for political refugees – where freedom of a political thought could be practised freely in a truly cosmopolitan intellectual milieu; and partly from a desire to avoid trouble in France's own Basque country where ethnic consciousness had traditionally been rather passive.

At the start of the 1980s, relations between France and Spain were still being soured on occasion by incidents which reflected divergent perspectives on how the security problem should be tackled. Bomb attacks on the Costa del Sol, for example, were alleged by the Spanish interior minister to have been planned in France; and there was an implied suggestion that the French authorities could have done more to keep a check on ETA sympathizers in south-western France. In the same year it was revealed that Spanish intelligence officers were working on French territory without the knowledge of the French government, and when this became apparent the French government protested by asserting that this was not the appropriate way to solve 'an internal Spanish problem'. As late as 1982, the French president paid an official visit to Spain, but the two sides were still unable to agree on a common policy, the French authorities still being unwilling to extradite Basque suspects to Spanish jurisdiction. From 1982 onwards, after the election of a Socialist government in Spain, it was possible to detect a shift in Franco–Spanish relations: there was more co-operation on the border, and France began deporting ETA suspects although not in the first instance to Spain but to other parts of the world. In January 1984, six ETA suspects were deported to Venezuela, and four others were assigned to live in other parts of France.

These developments were accompanied by the emergence of a new terrorist group (GAL), which specialized in murdering members of ETA residing in France. By the spring of 1984 GAL had claimed about half a dozen murders of Basques living in south-west France. The situation was further complicated when in response to the French government's co-operation with the Spanish authorities, a French Basque organization Iparretak began to attack tourist facilities in south-west France, and killed a policeman near Dax in August. In summer 1984, the French interior minister had visited Madrid to discuss ways of increasing co-operation between the two countries, the outcome being an undertaking by the French that ETA members involved in violence would be deported (although not necessarily to Spain) and by the Spanish that they would offer 'social reintegration' to any ETA members not wanted by the police in either country. A turning point came in August when a court in Pau ruled in favour of extradition to Spain of four ETA suspects, a decision that caused widespread protests in both the French and Spanish Basque regions. Throughout 1985 and 1986, further co-operation between the French and Spanish authorities acted like a pincer on ETA activists in the border region. ETA–M's 'military chief' was arrested in France in 1985 and deported to Gabon; and four ETA members were convicted in a French court of belonging to a 'criminal association', the first time this had ever been achieved inside France against ETA members. Soon the French police were handing over some ETA suspects directly to the Spanish police without any judicial proceedings, a sure sign of growing confidence between the two jurisdictions. On a visit to Spain as prime minister in November 1986, M. Chirac was thanked by Sr Gonzalez for the 'substantial advances' made in co-operation between the two countries.

Since 1980, the Spanish government has employed more accommodatory methods in its fight against terrorism. Realizing that a purely security response is unlikely to be totally successful, the Government has laid increasing emphasis on social reintegration and on political structures designed to give Basques a greater sense of involvement in their own region's administration. There are striking similarities between the Spanish experience and other analogous situations in Western Europe. The French government in Corsica and the British government in Northern Ireland have experimented with regional assemblies that are intended to bring the business of government closer to the elected representatives of the areas concerned. In all these regions governments have used emergency legislation and streamlined judicial procedures and have, in each case, run the risk of diluting the perceived legitimacy of the state. In both the Basque country and Northern Ireland co-operation with a neighbouring state has been an essential part of making the men of violence amenable to justice. In both these cases, and in Corsica, the task of the state's security forces has been made more difficult by the emergence of 'anti-terrorist terrorists' – groups whose aims are similar to those of the state but whose methods put them beyond the pale of the law, and thus equally the object of official condemnation. As we have seen, GAL arose in the Basque country as a group dedicated to the elimination of ETA activists, GAL has its own counterparts in Ulster's UVF, and Francia in Corsica.

As the annual death toll in the Basque country seems to have declined during the 1980s it appears that these more 'political' methods of dealing with ETA are meeting with success. As the habit of working within the region's institutions became more ingrained, the appeal of ETA may be on the wane. The broad ground-swell of support for Basque autonomy, as expressed in the electoral strength of the PNV and other like-minded parties, is unlikely to diminish given the real benefits of locally-determined economic policies. A comparison between Basque nationalism in France and in Spain underlines the fact that the latter's greater virulence is tied to perceptions of central government policies and in particular the economic balance of advantage in partly controlling the expenditure of tax revenues (Lancaster 1987). The same analysis argues that the strength of ethnic assertiveness in Spain's Basque country is largely a product of repressive policies under Franco's dictatorship, some of which involved economic penalties. The inauguration of more benevolent economic policies towards the region in the 1980s, in fact lowering the price that the Basques pay to be part of Spain, is likely to reduce further the cultural and political attachments to Basque nationalism. The pressure on the Basque language, due largely to an influx of non-Basque immigrants, seems likely to be but one reflection of declining ethnic militancy. Paradoxically, then, the key to the integration of peripheral nationalism in existing nation-states lies not in penalizing such peripheries, but in providing them with incentives for moderating their more extreme demands (Lancaster 1987). This task will not be easy since the restructuring of the Spanish economy, to make it more competitive, has involved traditional industries like shipbuilding that lie at the heart of Basque economic life. Indeed, it is possible that the resilience of ethnic sentiment in the Basque region may be due in part to unpopular economic policies being implemented by central government and it is, perhaps, a measure of Basque alienation from the rest of Spain that nationalist demands are the vehicle for essentially economic protests. At the same time, the collaboration between regional and national governments necessary to solve these issues is likely to remain elusive (Medhurst 1982: 14).

The political atmosphere in the Basque country remains brittle, and any allegations of brutality or illegality on the part of the security forces can undo months of patient work by the region's politicians. The support that ETA retains tends to fluctuate according to how the state administers the law. Like any government faced with a violent minority embedded in a broader society, the Spanish government has to walk the proverbial tightrope between those who pursue the constitutional road, and those who believe in the armed struggle, giving the former enough to sustain them without appearing to justify the methods of the latter.

A federal Spain?

The almost feverish haste surrounding the autonomy process was an instinctive reaction to the firm centralization of the Franco regime. By 1983, autonomy had been granted to seventeen regions each with its own capital city, flag, parliament, civil service, and supreme court. These regions not only vary considerably in size (Andalucía is ten times bigger than the Basque country) but the degree of autonomy achieved is much greater in some cases than in others. It is possible to distinguish four levels of autonomy: the Basques and Catalans at the top, the Andalucíans and Galicians on the second level, Valencia, Navarre, and the Canaries behind them, and all remaining regions at the lowest level. An attempt to harmonize the various forms of autonomy in a law, invariably known by its acronym LOAPA, was partly thwarted by the Spanish constitutional court in 1983 on the grounds that clauses guaranteeing state law supremacy over regional law, in areas where Galicia, Andalucía, the Basques, and Catalans had been given special competence, were unconstitutional. Something of a political mosaic has appeared in regional governments: whereas in Galicia, the Basque country and Catalonia a strong sense of ethnic identity is reflected in control by parties of a nationalist flavour, remaining regions have tended to follow the political swing towards the PSOE since 1982. A sense of identification with the Spanish state is intersected by strong ties of allegiance to regional governments: turnout in regional elections is usually high. The concept of the Spanish nation, something that has never been universally accepted in Spain, inevitably risks being further diluted as voters look to regional governments for bread-and-butter services, and to regional flags and other symbols for expressions of cultural distinctiveness. The word 'federal' has not been used very much to describe this new allocation of political power since it is feared that it will provoke reaction from those who treasure the 'sacred unity' of Spain. If federalism involves the constitutional allocation of functions to two distinct levels of government, then Spain has something very like a federal system. Disputes between the conflicting claims of central and regional governments are adjudicated upon by a constitutional court as happens in both West Germany and the United States. What distinguishes Spain from both those countries, however, is the lack of uniformity in the degree of autonomy granted to the seventeen regions. Furthermore, true federalism should avoid the notion of a 'centre': hence the selection of artificial capital cities like Bonn, Brasilia, Canberra, and Washington DC. Madrid cannot easily shake off its inheritance as the seat of a highly centralized government.

D.N. McIver (Williams 1982) has identified a serious problem, relevant to the Spanish case, that faces any state trying to cope with nationalist minority demands. In granting a degree of autonomy to an ethnic minority, the central government may be surrendering the means by which efficient administration is achieved. While a regional government may be more responsive to the needs of the population it administers, it may not have the means to remedy the problems it faces. Central government may have the means, but not be in a position to take the appropriate action because the functions have been delegated. 'The dilemma facing central authority is then that conceding special treatment and autonomous powers to ethnic minority groups may mean yielding some of the powers which central authorities themselves believe to be necessary to the uniform provision of effective government' (Williams 1982: 304). On the other hand, where a regional government successfully tackles a range of problems, the central government becomes less salient and residual loyalties may be deflected into an even stronger regional focus. This seems to be the case in Catalonia where the size, prosperity and efficiency of the regional administration have created 'a veritable state within a state' whose education, health and social services are distinctly superior to those in other parts of Spain (Hooper 1986: 264). The political unity of Spain can, however, only be put at risk by the success of experiments such as these in regional autonomy. If regional governments cost their electorates too much, if they become overloaded with self-seeking bureaucrats, if their performance is markedly inferior to what central government could provide, then the enthusiasm for autonomy will subside. What seems most likely is that the experience will be variable; and it may be that only the so-called 'historic nationalities' will want to hold on to their recently acquired self-government.

In a time of economic depression, one of the powers most eagerly sought by the regions is the ability to encourage industrial investment and stimulate job creation. On the whole, relations between Madrid and the regions have been co-operative and in cases where conflicts have occurred a constitutional tribunal has played a crucial role in demarcating the respective competences of the central and regional administrations. However, there is considerable tension of a horizontal kind which Spain's membership of the European Economic Community is likely to exacerbate. The poorer regions see themselves as dependent and exploited: they argue that they have contributed to Spain's development by providing labour and other resources and they argue that redistribution of resources via central government is essential to prevent the disintegration of national unity. The wealthier regions, the Basque country and Catalonia in particular, argue that the poorer regions are a drag on their own dynamic development and that by indulging the autonomist aspirations in these poorer areas the central state has established a series of parasitic mini-governments.

The Constitution provides for a system of cross-subsidization between regions. The Inter-territorial Compensation Fund, representing about 30 per cent of public capital investment (excluding defence), makes an allocation to all regions according to a weighted combination of per capita income, emigration, unemployment and surface area. Under this system, Extremadura, the poorest region, gets about thirty times as much per capita as Madrid, the richest area. These transfers have a high degree of visibility and are therefore the subject of intense political bargaining and controversy. The richer regions tend to be the more urbanized and they argue, understandably, that huge social problems in the cities deserve as much capital investment as the more dubious schemes for rejuvenating the rural wastelands of the south-west. The richer regions tend to be the nearest to the French border and the rest of the European Economic Community, while the poorest areas are on the Portuguese border in the far west. There is therefore a real gradient of wealth falling away westwards from the Pyrenees, a gradient that is likely to remain steep as the opportunities of a tariff-free market in the rest of Western Europe are seized most readily by the industrialized areas of Bilbao and Barcelona which, even before the Community came into existence, traditionally looked outside Spain for their commercial focus. As capital flows within the EEC are freed of all restrictions by 1992, the flow of foreign investment into the prosperous north-east of Spain will increase. These horizontal tensions between regions will accentuate a latent parochialism in Spanish politics that has managed to revive remarkably quickly in the last ten years despite its efficient and lengthy suppression under Franco's centralizing authoritarianism. Spain's membership of the EEC has thrust it into the grip of two converging processes: international economic integration but intra-national political disintegration (MacMillion 1981). This pessimistic interpretation sees multinational business deepening the regional economic imbalances within Spain and thereby deepening its political divisions; and as the country becomes more divided it is less able to withstand the economic onslaught from beyond its boundaries (indeed certain regions will entice international investment for their own benefit) and so the disintegration of the political cohesion of the state continues (Hudson and Lewis 1985: 297–308).

Chapter four
Women and politics: reflections of change

Introduction

The involvement of women in the Spanish political system since the restoration of democracy can be discussed from at least two perspectives. First, one can analyse the extent to which female voters have participated in elections, and which parties their votes have tended to favour. Second, a separate but related issue is the extent to which specifically women's issues have been taken on board by the political system. Clearly, the two perspectives may be related in as much as a high representation of women in the political system may result in feminine issues being more readily absorbed by the legislative process, but this is not necessarily the case. In this chapter we intend to examine both the participation of women in Spanish politics and the progress made in recognizing the broader rights of women in Spanish society.

Various powerful cultural forces in Spanish history have been suggested (Inglehart Reilly 1986) as reasons for the late advancement of Spanish women into political life. Seven centuries of Moorish rule left behind Islamic assumptions that women should be confined to their homes, and covered up completely in public. The fierce wars of the Reconquista inculcated a strongly fanatical version of Catholicism, epitomized by the Inquisition, and further emphasizing the subordinate role of women in Spanish society. The concomitant warrior tradition (personified by El Cid) exalted the quintessentially male virtues of valour, honour and chivalry while relegating to women the meeker virtues of chastity, modesty and humility. Socio-economic change and increasing secularization which in other parts of Western Europe had accompanied the Industrial Revolution, hardly affected Spain until the 1960s when the values of an essentially agricultural society began to be seriously questioned.

The demise of the Francoist dictatorship not only coincided with rapid economic changes that saw many more women in the workplace and in the lecture halls of universities, but it marked the beginning of the end of the Church's hegemony in ascribing to women a specific role in society. The dictatorship of General Franco did not end until 1975. Thus the tentative beginnings of democracy in Spain in the Second Republic (1931–9) were violently snuffed out by the civil war and then by forty years of authoritarian rule. Ironically, Spanish women voted for the first time in 1933, twelve years before women in France, and again in 1936, before losing all their political rights until 1977. Under the Franco dictatorship, women were expected to focus on domestic activities, and eschew public life with the sole exception of participation in the Seccion Femenina of the Falange. Women who refused to accept the subordinate role accorded to them by fascist society were branded as leftists; and this early identification of women's rights with the political left was the cornerstone of later political activity when feminist issues and other vogues such as anti-Americanism and pacifism became the property of the political left. In this respect, Spain was no different from the rest of Western Europe, it was simply that the process had been delayed by more than a decade due to the suppression of political debate until after Franco's death. In the 1960s, the new women's movement in Western Europe had been inspired by American role models and, like the movement in the United States, was part of a broader fermentation in society embracing civil rights, anti-war protest and a more permissive moral climate.

After the transition

After the transition to democratic politics, Spanish women were quick to participate in, and express an interest in, the political process. In the early 1980s the proportion of Spanish women who claimed that they were discussing politics 'sometimes' or 'often' with their friends was similar to levels recorded for Ireland, Italy and Belgium, but less than in West Germany, Britain or the Netherlands. This contrast may be explained by the impact of the Protestant Reformation (Inglehart Reilly 1986). The level of politicization among Spanish women is strongly influenced by education, by social class, and by whether or not the respondent is employed. In Eurobarometer surveys in 1982 and 1983 there is a marked contrast in politicization between women who left school at fifteen and those who remained in education beyond the age of nineteen. 'Only 34 per cent of the lower group ever talked about politics, compared to 74 per cent of the highly educated group, a difference of forty points'

(Inglehart Reilly 1986). As might be expected, and as is the case in other countries, higher social class is positively correlated with a greater degree of politicization. Clearly the differential extent of education goes some way towards explaining this. Inglehart Reilly found that, for both men and women, there was a similar increase in political awareness between the lower middle class and the middle class, but that for the next jump to upper middle class, the change was much more marked for women (Inglehart Reilly 1986: 22), an increase of 46 per cent and higher even than for men. Clearly these findings suggest that for women in elite positions, factors such as education have made them keenly aware of the unusual situation in which they find themselves, and they are therefore uniquely conscious of the political system that has made it possible. The effects of age on political awareness among West European women varies from country to country although it is broadly true that older women are politically more apathetic than younger women. In Spain the contrast is particularly strong. Young Spanish women aged 18 to 25 are twice as likely to discuss politics as women over the age of 65 (Inglehart Reilly 1986: 24).

Undoubtedly the effects of the civil war, and the forty-year dictatorship of General Franco, alienated a generation of Spaniards from the political process, and stifled the habit of openly discussing political events. Under Franco's rule, a variety of legal impediments discouraged women from taking up employment. Until 1975, a wife had to seek permission from her husband to embark on a number of activities outside the home: take a job, start a business, open a bank account, start legal proceedings or enter into legal contracts. From 1976, the proportion of women rose steadily but settled at about 30 per cent of those employed in the early 1980s, a level lower than in many other West European countries. The impact of employment on women's politicization is more marked than in most other parts of Western Europe: one study reckons that there is a 20 per cent difference in the degree of politicization between women who work and those who do not, whereas Irish women are relatively apathetic politically whether or not they work, and West German women tend to be highly politicized irrespective of their employment status (Inglehart Reilly 1986: 27). For many Spanish women, the experience of paid employment is new; and it is the younger women who are most anxious to seek jobs. This experience, coupled with rising educational qualifications and a more sceptical outlook on conventional Catholic teaching on the role of women in society, seems bound to stimulate a political awareness comparable to that found in other West European societies.

These observations are reinforced when one considers female

participation in Spanish elections. There is hardly any gender gap in electoral turnout: a difference of about 5 per cent at the most in the early 1980s has been noted by one writer, who adds that the 'practical rather than ideological nature of women's abstention negated predictions that they would form an uninterested, apolitical or indifferent grouping' (Abel and Torrents 1984: 140). In common with other Western countries, a gender gap in political preferences has been noticeable in Spain. First, self-identification on a right–left scale finds women and men slightly left of centre by the mid-1980s, with women typically slightly less left-inclined than men. This contrasts with Ireland (Fogarty, Ryan and Lee 1984) and West Germany (Conradt 1986), for example, where ideological self-identification tends to cluster to the right of centre (although less so for West Germany than Ireland). Second, when we look at voting patterns, these indicate a drift to the left in the 1980s among both men and women but with women typically less likely to support left-wing parties than men. In 1979, there was a 12 per cent gender gap in the voting for parties on the left, and 13 per cent for parties on the right; in 1982 these gaps had narrowed to 10 per cent and 5 per cent respectively (Abel and Torrents 1984: 143). When one looks at the gender composition of each party's supporters, we see the usual preference for right and centre parties for women voters. The UCD was especially strongly supported by women – 59 per cent of their vote in 1979 – while the Communist party (PCE) attracted 65 per cent male support in the same election. The PSOE attracted almost equal shares of its vote from men and women, with a slight bias towards male voters, while about two-thirds of the Coalición Democratica's vote was female (Abel and Torrents 1984: 144).

To what extent are women represented in the Spanish political system? The political system itself has inevitably expanded with the advent of democracy, and it would be surprising if women had not benefited from this. Between 1981 and 1982, a woman was a cabinet minister for the first time since the Civil War; and the PSOE government appointed no fewer than thirteen women to ministerial positions during the first term of office. Overall, female representation in the Cortes has settled at about 6 per cent, a level comparable with many other West European countries, but considerably lower than in Scandinavia (Norris 1987). In the mid-1980s, 8 per cent of councillors, and 6 per cent of the members of autonomous parliaments, were female (Threlfall 1985: 69). In the 1986 elections, women took 23 of the 350 seats in the lower house (6.6 per cent), ten out of 208 seats in the Senate (4.8 per cent), which compares with an overall 6.3 per cent in the Cortes between 1982 and 1986. In the European Parliament there are six female MEPs out of a total of 60 from Spain, three in the Socialist Group, one in the European People's Party, one in the European Democrats, and one non-aligned.

Public opinion appears to be moving, however, towards greater representation for women in the political system. In a survey published by the Minister of Culture in 1986, three-quarters of respondents felt that women should play a greater part in political life. However, 58 per cent said that women were 'not sufficiently prepared' for a political career; 79 per cent said that the parties preferred male candidates; and two-thirds of respondents blamed women for not being forceful enough in demanding a say in politics. Moreover, more than two-thirds of all respondents agreed that a career in politics is compatible with a woman's family responsibilities, and disagreed that 'politics is not for women' (Women of Europe 1986: 29). As recently as 1987 another survey confirmed these findings: over 65 per cent of respondents wanted to see more women in government and in the legislature (Women of Europe 1987: 28–9). Compared with other West European countries, moreover, Spanish public opinion appears to be slightly more well-disposed to the idea of women in politics than Luxembourg, Belgium, Greece, Portugal, and West Germany, but less so than other EEC countries. In response to the assertion that 'Politics should be left to men', Luxembourgers (34 per cent) were most in agreement and the Danes (7 per cent) the least, with Spain (24 per cent) quite close to the Community mean of 22 per cent (Eurobarometer 1987).

Legislative reforms

The Spanish Constitution of 1978 paved the way for a number of reforms that were to affect women directly. The Constitution provided a framework within which equal treatment for women became regarded as a legal requirement and not as something intrinsically threatening to the social order. The Constitution not only states that all Spaniards are equal before the law (Article 14) but refers specifically to their 'right to work' and to 'a free choice of occupation or activity, to promotion through work and to remuneration sufficient to meet their needs and those of their family' and that they 'shall in no circumstances be subjected to discrimination based on sex' (Article 35). The Constitutional Court has refined these laudable but general statements. In 1981 the court ruled that unequal treatment was not always discriminatory; in 1983 it ruled that equality was not an absolute principle, that objective factors could exist that justified unequal treatment, especially where the aim was 'to help restore or promote real equality'.

In 1980, the constitutional principle of non-discrimination in relation to work was embedded in the Workers' Statute and the Basic Law on Employment. This document covered several aspects of potential discrimination against women: criteria for promotion had to be the same for both sexes; pay had to be the same for the same work; and working conditions had to be the same for male and female employees. At the same time the Government committed itself to the adoption of special training programmes aimed at fostering employment for workers facing special difficulties in gaining access to the labour market, especially 'women with family responsibilities' (Article 38.2 of the Basic Law on Employment).

The Constitution, and legislation subsequently enacted, has also emphasized equality between men and women within marriage. New legislation on the family in 1981 provided for the joint authority of husband and wife over their children. This, and other similar legislation, was a logical extension of the Constitution's general statement that 'men and women are entitled to enter into marriage on a basis of full legal equality' (Article 32.1). In the public sphere, the Constitution treats women and men as equals. Both come of age at eighteen (Article 12). All citizens (therefore men and women equally) 'have the right to participate in public affairs, directly or through their representatives freely elected in periodic elections by universal suffrage' and 'they likewise have the right to accede on equal terms to public functions and offices, in accordance with the requirements to be prescribed by law' (Article 23). On two major issues, the Constitution deliberately remained silent, as if to leave the door open for legislative change: abortion and divorce. These two issues are now considered.

Although stiff penalties were attached to the crime of abortion under the Franco regime, it has been estimated that about 300,000 abortions were carried out annually in the mid-1970s. While most Spanish women procured back-street abortions with all the attendant dangers, both legal and medical, middle-class women were able to afford abortions at private clinics in foreign cities such as London. One-eighth of all abortions carried out in England and Wales are carried out on Spanish passport holders (Hooper 1987: 191). The prevalence of abortion in Spain has been associated with the difficulties in obtaining proper contraception: condoms were available illegally and the Pill only became available in the early 1970s and then only in its guise as a remedial measure for pre-menstrual tension and other hormonal disorders. A sufficient number of doctors were willing to connive at this so that by 1975, the year Franco died, half a million women were using the Pill in Spain (Hooper 1987: 189). The sale of contraceptives was made legal in 1978, but their availability and the knowledge required to make them effective was still sadly lacking. In 1982, among fifteen developed countries analysed, Spain had the lowest percentage of married women (aged 15–44) using contraception of some kind (Norris 1987: 98); hence a continuing high level of abortions among Spanish women (one abortion for every two live births by the early 1980s).

Pressure to have the law reformed gained strength in the period following the return of democratic government. Familiar tactics such as self-denunciation (publicly admitting to have had, or helped someone else to have, an abortion) attracted media attention in 1979 and 1980. Police had to forcibly evict 300 women who occupied a court building in Madrid where eleven Bilbao women were being tried for carrying out abortions (Hooper 1987: 191). Despite the high level of publicity these cases aroused, public opinion remained unconvinced that the law on abortion should be liberalized. In late 1982, a survey among women in Spain showed that 55 per cent were against abortion in all cases, 24 per cent were in favour in some circumstances, and 18 per cent were in favour in all circumstances. In 1983, when the Government introduced its law on abortion, 57 per cent said they were in favour of the 'Government's decision' to allow abortion in certain cases, and between 56 per cent and 66 per cent agreed when these cases were spelled out in detail. Women were marginally less in favour than men (Threlfall 1985: 65). The law of 1983 allowed the decriminalization of abortion in only three circumstances: the need to avoid grave danger to the life or health of the mother; a pregnancy resulting from a rape that had been reported to the police and only if performed during the first trimester; or a prognosis by two specialists that the foetus was likely to be born with serious physical or mental disability, and only if the abortion took place during the first 22 weeks. Although the bill was passed by 186 votes to 109 in the Congress of Deputies, and 110 to 45 in the Senate, it was prevented from coming into effect for a further two years by its reference to the Constitutional Court by the Alianza Popular on the grounds that it contravened Article 15 of the Constitution which states that 'all have the right to life and to physical and moral integrity'. The word 'all' had in fact replaced 'all persons' in an earlier draft of the constitution, specifically to leave open the possibility of a debate on the abortion issue (Bonime-Blanc 1987: 97). It was not until April 1985 that the Court ruled against the Government, saying that the law would have to be rewritten to specify more clearly how it would operate in practice. In the meantime, in July 1984, the Court overturned a sentence of one month's imprisonment passed on a woman who had had an abortion in England. The Government succeeded in piloting an amended abortion bill through the Cortes in the summer of 1985, and its provisions came into force on 2 August. In its new form the bill allowed an abortion after a rape, provided the abortion was carried out within 12 weeks; and in cases of malformation of the foetus, the termination had to be performed within 22 weeks. Abortions had to be carried out in designated clinics, by a qualified person and the permission of another doctor (another two doctors in cases of foetus malformation) had to be obtained. In addition, the law was drawn more widely to take into account the mental and physical health of the mother in cases where this was the ground for termination. In June 1985, the Spanish bishops announced that any woman having an abortion, or any person performing one, would be excommunicated. The liberalization of the abortion law in Spain has resulted in fewer Spanish women travelling to England for their terminations. In late 1986, a decree allowing private clinics to carry out abortions was held in abeyance while the Constitutional Court deliberated on it, following a case brought by the Spanish Life Movement.

Until 1981, when Spain introduced a law on divorce, there was no way to end a marriage in Spain except by an annulment. Strictly speaking, annulments ought not to have been easy to achieve, requiring as they did evidence of non-consummation, or lack of free will in entering the marriage contract. However, thousands of couples did obtain annulments although the preponderance of rich or influential couples who succeeded in clearing the various ecclesiastical hurdles inevitably aroused suspicions that there was one law for the rich and one for the poor. For those who could not afford an annulment, there was the possibility of a legal separation. This, however, was a lengthy process, sometimes taking years, and often prohibitively costly in terms of legal fees. The process required there to be a 'guilty partner'; the guilt had to be proved in a court of law, and the guilty partner lost all chances of custody or alimony. At the end of the Franco period, there were hundreds of thousands of couples living in marriages that had lost all meaning; and it was not therefore surprising that, in 1975, over 70 per cent of people questioned in a poll said they were in favour of divorce being made legal (Hooper 1987: 199).

Between 1977 and 1981, the drafting of an acceptable divorce law became a major political issue. On the one hand, there was strong opposition from the Church and the political right; on the other hand there was support for such a bill from the PSOE and from women's groups who not only favoured divorce but were concerned that no law would have meaning unless it was backed up with ways of making sure that financial obligations after a divorce were properly enforced by the courts. In 1980 the justice minister in the UCD government, Sr Ordoñez, introduced his bill on divorce: it allowed divorce in less than two years, there was no need for guilt to be apportioned, and there was scope for a divorce by mutual consent of the partners. The bill proved to be the most contentious issue facing the UCD coalition and eventually led to its downfall. The Christian Democrat wing of the party had grave reservations about the proposed legislation and their hand was strengthened by both the abortive military coup in February 1981 (which shifted the party to the right) and by the known disapproval of the law by the Pope. Ordoñez piloted the bill through the Cortes, but it came near to being amended in the Senate in a way which would have given the judge in a divorce case the right to stop the divorce if he felt that it was injurious to one of the parties or to the children. The law, essentially in its original form, came into effect on 7 July 1981, but not before the Spanish bishops warned that the new law 'gravely disturbs the stability of marriage and, moreover, leaves to such a large extent the decision over ending the marriage to the partners themselves'. The controversy surrounding the passage of the bill through the Cortes had severed the UCD coalition irreparably and the ensuing election saw the demise of the UCD for good. 'The issue which, above all others, sealed its fate was divorce' (Hooper 1987: 201).

Besides opening the floodgates to a large number of divorces that had been waiting patiently to be consummated, the new law produced doubts as to whether or not it was a clear victory for women. The fact that fewer women than men supported divorce legislation was a reflection of doubts about the enforceability of alimony judgements, doubts which have not been entirely laid to rest. On the other hand it is more often women than men who initiate divorce proceedings in Spain suggesting that many see divorce as the lesser of two evils open to them (Threlfall 1985: 61) when the alternative may be a philandering husband or domestic violence. Half of all divorces in Spain are instigated by wives alleging cruelty on the part of their husbands (Threlfall 1985: 61). By the mid-1980s, however, one in five of Spanish marriages was ending in divorce although this was still a lower rate than in many other West European countries. Nevertheless, rising divorce rates result in women becoming vulnerable to poverty, and to all the kindred disadvantages of single parenthood, since two-thirds of all divorces in Western Europe involve dependent children (Norris 1987: 82). All this leads many Spanish feminists to question whether any kind of divorce is really advantageous for women.

Spanish feminism

It will be seen from what has been said so far that in the period 1977–84 several important legislative changes were effected that dramatically altered the position of women in Spanish society. We turn now to consider the role of the women's movement in Spain since the end of the Franco dictatorship. Lovenduski (1986) has argued that 'second-wave feminism' was characterized by the complementarity of separate strategies within the broader movement. Thus while radical feminists have set up autonomous organizations to act as counter-cultural alternatives to the established patriarchal norms in West European society, their liberal sisters have campaigned through the trade unions, the political parties, and other interest groups for change within the system. The impact of the former groups has been that of 'consciousness-raising' while that of the latter has been to translate new awareness among women into acceptable legislative reforms. In Spain the women's movement has been marginal to the mass of women in Spanish society, playing the role of *agent provocateur* but ultimately less influential than the media, the opinion polls and the political parties. Spanish feminists have been 'a ferment, a symbol, but also a distant mirror in which most Spanish women do not recognize themselves' (Dahlerup 1986: 204).

One writer (Threlfall 1985) has identified at least three historic disadvantages that impeded the development of an active, coherent, and influential women's movement after the demise of the Franco dictatorship in 1975. In the first place the overwhelming priority during the 'transition' was the establishment of democracy and, on the left, there was some feeling that campaigning on women's issues was a distraction from this more important antecedent goal. Thus feminists became what Threlfall calls an 'opposition within the opposition' pleading for the same kind of enlightenment within the left that the left itself was struggling for in the broader political arena. Second, Spanish feminists had no substantial record of previous achievement on which to draw for inspiration since the major advances for women, such as the granting of the vote, constitutional equality, divorce, and abortion had all been granted in the 1930s as a result of conflict between right-and left-wing political parties, not by feminists *per se*; and all these rights had, in any case, been quickly extinguished by Franco's victory in the civil war. A third obstacle was an understandable aversion, on the part of those most anxious to see the realization of women's rights, to segregated women's movements, since these were uncomfortably reminiscent of the Falange's Seccion Femenina whose task it had been to inculcate the Hispanic equivalents of *Kirche, Kuche, Kinder* into a whole generation of Spanish women.

After the elections of 1977, the liberating atmosphere of democratic political activity nurtured a widespread upsurge of interest in feminist issues across the country. Women's groups sprang up not only in the large cities but even in smaller towns where progressive forms of politics had not previously been conspicuous. The election of women, some of them committed feminists, to the Cortes in 1977 meant that for the first time women's views were being heard from within the political system as well as from outside it. This led to the debate on *doble militancia*, the debate between those who felt that women's oppression should be fought from within a political party as well as from the ranks of the women's movement. The parties of the left, the PSOE and PCE, were most susceptible to women's issues; and were most likely to attract female candidates. As the political system appeared willing, in principle at least, to address itself to the major legislative reforms necessary to achieve equality between men and women with regard to marital law and employment, the scores of women's groups that were established throughout Spain tended to focus on specifically female concerns such as contraception, abortion and rape. Advice centres helped women to arrange abortions, often abroad, and proffered a range of gynaecological services. Refuges for battered wives were able to operate more freely in the wake of more liberal legislation regarding the rights of wives to leave the family home (in Franco's time, a wife leaving the family home even for a few days without her husband's permission was breaking the law).

The text of the new Constitution itself laid foundations on which the Spanish feminist movement could build its case for equality in a wide range of spheres. In its assertion that there was to be no discrimination on grounds of birth, race, sex, religion or political view, the Constitution provided a virtually open door for feminists to push against. Although the 1931 Constitution had enshrined the equality of men and women, the forty-year dictatorship had turned the clock back so far that, in the late 1970s, the mood was one of making up for lost time. Feminists were divided on the Constitution itself: was it enough to welcome it on the grounds that it provided a context within which feminists would find their legislative battles easier to fight, or did the Constitution's failure to confront issues like divorce and abortion render it unworthy of feminist support? Clearly many radical feminists took the latter view.

In 1979 a congress of the feminist movement was convened in Granada to which 3,000 delegates came. The two principal ideological streams proved irreconcilable, and the meeting ended in disagreements and divisions. The dichotomy, common to other feminist movements in Western Europe, separating those who saw women as being distinct as a gender from those who saw them as merely equal, and dividing those who believed that the struggle should be carried on within the political parties from those who sought to change the whole system from without, was never really bridged in Spain. The movement lost even its superficial coherence and, from 1980 onwards, had no great battles to fight, except that of abortion. Many women 'decided on personal transformation as the only road to liberation' (Dahlerup 1986: 212). The political system, by accommodating many of its earlier demands, had effectively spiked the guns of the mainstream feminist movement. In addition, the regionalization of the political system, as autonomous governments were established, made a centralized national organization less attractive and less necessary. Henceforth, the women's movement mirrored the regional focus of political activity.

The apparent disintegration of organized feminism in Spain should not be taken as a sign of weakness, but as a sign of its resilience. If new-wave feminism is analysed as a social movement, its amorphous organizational structure is not perceived as a disability. For the sake of argument we can characterize a social movement as a collective attempt to promote social change with a minimum of organization by relying heavily on the commitment of activists. The constant rise and fall of loosely interconnected groups gives the feminist movement its special resilience: its flexibility is a strength when it makes contact with the more rigid structures of the state. 'It is because women are marginal to the political system and women's causes are seen as peripheral that it has been necessary for feminists to opt for social movement forms' (Lovenduski 1986: 66). Lovenduski's rider that the ultimate goal of feminism must be 'change in the way politics and the role of the state is conceptualized', and that the lack of this qualitative change may be obscured by apparently reformist legislation, is particularly pertinent in the Spanish case.

Public attitudes towards the role of women in Spanish society have changed rapidly since 1975, and these changes have effectively removed much of the sense of urgency that characterized the earlier stages of the feminists' campaign. In a survey of 2,100 respondents, published in 1975, there was overwhelming evidence of public support for the notion of gender roles. The survey showed that 82 per cent agreed that 'household jobs should be done by women; the husband should only do them when his wife is sick'; 79 per cent agreed that the 'woman must be at home when her husband gets in from work'; and 68 per cent felt that a 'woman's training should fit her for looking after her family rather than going out to work'. Significantly, there was not much discrepancy between male and female responses to these questions: there was a broad acceptance by women that their role was that of 'supporter' and 'home-maker'. Interestingly, the only contrasts in the responses were according to age, with younger respondents of both sexes much less willing to accept the traditional division of duties between husband and wife. That changing attitudes were already appearing is confirmed by another survey, published in 1979, and covering 5,000 households across Spain. Here, two-thirds of those polled agreed that 'women should go out to work just as men do' and there was higher support among women for this than among men (73 per cent to 62 per cent). However, these levels of support for the 'working woman' conceal reservations among male respondents relating to particular cases: 47 per cent thought that if the husband earned enough to keep his wife, the wife should not go out to work; 58 per cent thought that a mother with young children should not put the children into a daycare centre and go out to work, but stay at home and look after them. We can supplement these findings by another survey (in 1980) which asked married couples how tasks were shared in the home. In 88 per cent of cases the wife alone was responsible for cleaning the house, in 86 per cent of cases for washing up, in 75 per cent of cases for getting the breakfast, in 66 per cent of cases for feeding the children, but in only 31 per cent of homes for doing household repairs.

In 1987, according to the results of a Eurobarometer poll, traditionally attributed marital roles in the Spanish home seem to undergo a significant change. Asked to choose between three definitions of 'ideal roles of husband and wife in the family', respondents were offered a couple where each partner has an equally absorbing job and share the housework and child-rearing equally, a couple where the wife has a less demanding job and does most of the housework and child-rearing, and a couple where the husband has a job and the wife runs the home. In Spain the choices were 47 per cent, 19 per cent and 28 per cent, respectively, compared to the EEC averages of 41 per cent, 29 per cent, and 25 per cent (Eurobarometer 1987).

It is perhaps both a symptom and a cause of these attitudinal changes that the Spanish state has, in a very direct sense, co-opted a large part of the feminist movement by the creation of the Instituto de la Mujer. Established by the PSOE government out of an obscure sub-department in the Ministry of Culture in 1983, and headed by Carlota Bustelo, a committed feminist and PSOE deputy elected in 1977, the institute saw its budget rise ten-fold in the first year of its existence: by 1985, it was dealing with a budget of £3.5 million. The main purpose of the institute has been to advance the cause of women within the framework of the Constitution. It cannot reach beyond the policies of the government and thus it falls short of the expectations of the more radical feminists (Dahlerup 1986: 214). As a strategy for promoting the idea that the government was 'doing something' about the position of women in Spanish society, it has been rather effective. Among its activities are courses for civil servants and senior police officers, and numerous seminars often held in conjunction with an academic institution. The institute has published numerous booklets, leaflets, and studies that give advice, illuminate inadequacies, and alert women to the opportunities open to them. In two areas, in particular, the institute has been busy: the promotion of employment among women and the adaptation of Spanish laws to the norms prevailing in the European Economic Community. In the autumn of 1987, for example, the institute and the European Commission in Madrid co-sponsored a two-day seminar on the topic of equal opportunities. The extent to which the institute tries to assert its independence of government, despite its financial dependence on it, emerged at the seminar when the institute's director, Ms Bustelo, drew attention to the gulf between the constitutional rights of women and the everyday reality they were experiencing: and warned that 'state pseudo-feminism' could not be tolerated. The institute's monthly magazine *Mujeres* is a mine of information relating to the status of women in Spain. The institute has also spawned a network of information centres, of which there were eleven by the end of 1987, in places as far apart as Las Palmas in the Canaries, Seville in Andalucía, and Santander in the Basque country. The fact that, in one month alone (September 1986), 4,442 women used these advice centres suggests that they are very much needed.

In the mid-1980s a wide range of groups existed in Spain that were wholly or partly devoted to the advancement of women's interests. The Coordinadora Estatal linked together feminist groups that were associated to non-parliamentary parties; and under its aegis there existed both feminist study groups and lesbian collectives. By contrast, a feminist party was established in 1984, based in Barcelona, and has been firmly attached to the idea that feminists must capture the citadels of political power if anything is to change. Within the existing political parties, spokespersons, caucuses and special groups exist for women. Both the major trade union federations, the UGT and the Comisiónes Obreras, have women's groups. The Roman Catholic Church supports a network of women's groups throughout the country whose role is rather ambivalent, at least from a feminist perspective. While on the one hand these groups seem designed to keep women mindful of their appropriate role in society, the mere

existence of the groups, especially in rural areas, can help to stimulate female collective consciousness. The Alianza Popular has its
Association of Conservative Women which aims to preserve the best
of traditional values while not neglecting women's role in modern
society. In addition to all these more general groups, there exist
countless others that provide specific services for women and may or
may not necessarily be feminist in outlook: abortion advice centres,
literacy groups, rape counselling services, refuges for battered wives,
birth control clinics, and groups that specialize in advising and help-
ing widows, single mothers, divorcees, prostitutes and female
prisoners.

What kind of women have been active in the feminist movement
in Spain? Largely from her own experience, Threlfall (1985) has
identified three types of women that get involved in feminist activity.
First, there is a group of middle-class, professional women in their
thirties or forties, usually living in Madrid or Barcelona, and often
with a university education. Second, there is a younger group of
usually single women, middle-class, career-oriented, who live an almost bohemian lifestyle defying easy categorization into
conventional class terms but aspiring to be upwardly mobile. Third,
there are those who are often the recipients of help or advice, having
experienced divorces, abortions, rape or marital violence, and have
become absorbed into the movement by virtue of what it has done for
them. By definition, these women do not belong to any particular social class. Indeed, they, like many feminists in Spain, would ask
whether conventional class labels are relevant to women since these
labels so often relate to a man's occupation. If a 'middle-class' woman
suddenly finds herself a single parent she may well become more like
a working-class person as far as her economic resources are concerned, although her educational and personal attributes still place
her in a middle-class bracket.

As a group in Spanish society, feminists have traditionally been a
minority within womanhood and have had little in common with the
rest of their sex. What has distinguished feminists from other women
in Spain has been their relatively less firm attachment to religion,
their higher level of educational achievement, and the likelihood that
they live in an urban as opposed to a rural environment. However, as
the availability of educational and employment opportunities
spreads to more women, and as the state itself reinterprets the norms
of society so that feminist goals assume an almost mundane quality,
the dichotomy between the feminist 'vanguard' and the 'mass' of
Spanish women will become increasingly blurred.

It is perhaps a sign of how far the rights of women have been incorporated into Spanish law during the past decade that the

Constitutional Court has recently begun to set limits to the scope of equal opportunities. In one recent case a widow was prevented from receiving a pension because she had never been married to the man with whom she had cohabited for forty years, and whose three children she had borne. The court ruled that 'marriage and cohabitation out of wedlock are not equivalent situations'. In another case, the court rejected an appeal from a Sr Navarro who argued that, under Article 41 of the Constitution, he was, as the father of a two-year old girl, entitled to the same child benefit that was paid to mothers working in the same hospital as he did (Women of Europe No. 51 1987: 28–9).

Legal interpretations of the Constitution's broad provisions relating to equality between the sexes provide one source of pressure for change. The membership of Spain in the European Economic Community provides another. As Spain moves through the transitional phase towards full membership, any incompatibilities between its national laws and the EEC law will have to be removed. When a country joins the EEC, it agrees to abide by all existing EEC laws as well as any new laws that may be made in the future. With this obligation in mind, the Spanish government has announced a 'medium-term plan' (1987–90) designed to bring Spanish national law into line with that of the EEC. The declared goals of the plan encompass virtually every aspect of women's place in Spanish society: to translate the broad provisions of the Constitution into national legislation; to provide women with adequate access to education, information and culture; to encourage a better balance in the sharing of parental responsibilities within the family; to enable men and women to take free and responsible decisions with regard to parenthood; to provide better health facilities specifically for women; to diversify the academic and career opportunities open to girls; to expand the proportion of women in employment and reduce the amount of occupational segregation by gender; to extend the social welfare protection for the most disadvantaged women; to increase participation by women in politics, and their representation in government and administration; and to carry out more research into the status of women in Spanish society and ways in which it can be enhanced. This last objective has already been given an important start by the publication, in 1987, of a 1,000-page study into the position of women in Spain today. Entitled *Situación Social de la Mujer en España*, this encyclopedic work discusses, amongst other things, family structure, educational opportunities, employment prospects, feminine health, political attitudes and voting behaviour among Spanish women, and the impact of the EEC.

Chapter five
Foreign policy: ambiguous change

Introduction

Foreign policy has been defined as 'the range of actions taken by varying sections of the government of a state in its relations with other bodies similarly acting on the international stage, supposedly in order to advance the national interest' (Reynolds 1980). The term 'national interest' is taken to refer to the overall interest of a specific national society, its survival and the maximization of its welfare. It goes without saying that although various national objectives at any given time are mutually incompatible (e.g. Britain's desire to preserve commercial independence but at the same time derive benefits from its membership of the European Economic Community), each is justifiable in terms of serving the national interest, and each is seen as a means to achieve an end.

Foreign policy can be distinguished from domestic policy in a number of ways. Foreign policy requires a greater willingness to adapt one's own objectives to accommodate the objectives of others. Foreign policy is rarely a complete success or a complete failure: in fact, it is rarely complete. It consists for the most part of actions taken to advance general broad goals but the goals are not likely to be totally achievable, and success can be measured only by the distance travelled along the road towards the intended destination. Foreign policy is subject to no binding laws; and is much more constrained by power relationships than is domestic policy. It is, finally, more vulnerable to factors that are unforeseen, unexpected and unmanageable.

The making of foreign policy is moulded by traditions, culture and style that are peculiar to a country. The geographical location of a country, its size, its neighbours and its distance from or proximity to theatres of conflict all contribute to the way its government perceives the outside world and orders its priorities. Its capacity for action, and its ability to withstand pressure from other states, will be determined by its indigenous resources, energy, self-sufficiency, availability of raw materials and the degree to which it can feed its inhabitants from domestic sources. These considerations will define the country's vulnerability to economic blockades or other more subtle forms of economic pressure exerted by other states. Internally, government cohesion and the stability of the political system will lay the foundations for a foreign policy that is credible; just as substantial ethnic minorities with external allegiances can undermine that same credibility by allowing 'the tail to wag the dog' as the Jewish lobby is sometimes able to do in the United States. Foreign policy is not made in a vacuum: it has to take account of various domestic interests like those of farmers, trade unionists, consumers, industrialists, or political parties, just as it has to accommodate the realities of the international scene. 'The foreign Minister . . . has to weave motifs dear to his own heart onto a tapestry on which many other hands are busily working' (Northedge 1974: 17). One might extend this analogy by saying that the overall design of the tapestry cannot be ignored, but the national contribution must nevertheless be pleasing to those whose interests it represents.

Foreign policy activities fall into two main categories: those that are reactive and those that are pre-emptive. States are constantly attempting to pre-empt developments that they perceive may be injurious to the national interest. They join alliances to maximize their security; they issue warnings to ward off potential enemies; they seek to avoid dependence upon supply routes that may be vulnerable to interdiction. When pre-emptive policies fail, reactive policies take over. Naval task forces are dispatched to win back territory that has been snatched by an invader; bombs are dropped on countries that refuse to surrender; and blockades are imposed on shipping lanes along which arms are carried to a neighbouring country with hostile intentions.

Spanish foreign policy

We begin our discussion by considering the context in which Spanish foreign policy is made. Geographically, Spain is clearly attached to Western Europe but its political leanings before 1975, its imperial ambitions in, and lingering nostalgia for, Latin America, and its cultural ties to the American hemisphere all conspired to keep Spain detached in spirit from Western Europe until the restoration of democracy in the late 1970s. After the loss of its last American colonies in 1898, Spain's foreign policy became restricted to the

Mediterranean and North Africa, and even here she was not a major actor. In the twentieth century, Spain's isolation was made virtually complete by the long-lasting regime of General Franco (1939–75) during which the country's 'pariah' status was relieved only by an alliance with the United States and a concordat with the Vatican. Spain was not admitted to the United Nations until 1955, or to the Council of Europe until 1977. Today, one of the principal motivations behind Spain's membership of both the European Economic Community and the North Atlantic Treaty Organization is the belief that forces supportive of democracy in Spain will be anchored more firmly in these broader groupings.

The advent of democracy in Spain after 1978 has clearly altered the domestic context in which foreign policy is made. The Constitution reveals some concern with foreign policy in so far as it involves the Cortes in the signature of treaties, and places some constraints on the types of treaties to which the country may become a party. The possibility of holding a referendum on foreign policy issues is not excluded by the Constitution in Article 92. In the period since 1978, there has been a decidedly healthy tendency in Spain for foreign policy issues to be widely aired in the media, in the Cortes, in the trade unions, in the universities and in the political parties. The debate that preceded the NATO referendum best epitomized this new enthusiasm for public debate in the foreign policy arena. But it was not the only example. Gibraltar, nuclear weapons, the North African enclaves, relations with Latin America, East–West relations and Spain's adaptation to the EEC all feature heavily in media treatment of foreign affairs. The creation of the autonomous communities adds a further dimension to the elaboration of foreign policy within Spain. The statute of the Basque country, for example, allows the regional government to make agreements with foreign governments provided these do not exceed the limits imposed by the national Constitution. Foreign policy thus provides additional possibilities for disagreement, and even tension, between the government in Madrid and the regional governments (Pollack 1987: 114).

Spain's bilateral relationship with the United States has been the central feature of its foreign policy since the dictatorship of Franco. In the early 1950s, Spain and the United States found that they had complementary interests. Franco's government was anxious to break out of the diplomatic isolation resulting from his victory in the civil war (1936–9) and the United States was keen to fill the strategic 'gap' left by Spain in the western defences. Both Portugal and France were full members of NATO and both the size and position of Spain made it an obvious site for American military and air force bases. The agreements signed between the two countries in 1953 provided Spain with both military and economic aid, and an end to diplomatic isolation. In return, the United States were given four bases over which they had virtually sovereign control: Rota, Torrejon, Zaragoza, and Moron. Up until 1970, the Americans had a virtual *carte blanche* as to how they used the bases; and the military and economic aid given to Spain in return was meagre by comparison with the military advantages derived by the Americans from these footholds in the Iberian peninsula. For Franco, the principal benefit was not economic but diplomatic: he now had an important bilateral relationship with the leading superpower bestowing a degree of respectability on his regime that had been conspicuously lacking hitherto.

In the post-Franco period the American bases have become something of an embarrassment. First, they are a constant reminder of the lengths to which Franco was prepared to go in order to legitimize his regime. Second, they have involved Spain in nuclear weaponry in as much as Polaris submarines visited Rota (near Cadiz) until forbidden to do so under an agreement made in 1976, and implemented in 1979. Third, there exists in Spain little enthusiasm for United States foreign policy in Latin America: Spanish public opinion supports the Argentinian claim to the Falklands; and was opposed to the assistance being given to the Contras in Nicaragua. Fourth, it is difficult to convince Spaniards that their country is seriously threatened by the Warsaw Pact: there is a strong neutralist strand in public opinion that argues against Spanish involvement in Cold War alliances and believes that Spanish national security is actually jeopardized by the presence of American bases.

Spain and NATO

The controversy over the American bases continues, but the context of the argument has been changed since 1982 by the entry of Spain into the North Atlantic Treaty Organization. The decision to enter the alliance was taken in the dying months of the UCD government under Sotelo. Neither seeking consensus for the decision nor arguing cogently for it, the UCD government had hoped vainly that Spanish entry into NATO would speed up the negotiations for Spanish entry into the EEC. Even if this argument had proved correct, which it was not, it is doubtful if many voters on the Left would have approved Sotelo's decision to ignore requests from the Socialists (PSOE) for a referendum on this crucial issue.

When the PSOE came to power in the 1982 elections they found themselves leading a country that was not yet a member of the EEC, but was now a member of NATO. Yet, as a party, the PSOE would have wished exactly the reverse. To many, it must have seemed an anomalous situation: Spain was already in a bilateral relationship with the United States that purported to protect Spain against a threat which was far from imminent while it gave no protection against what many regarded as a greater danger, namely the possibility of Morocco taking the Spanish-controlled enclaves of Ceuta and Melilla (in North Africa) by force. To straighten out the anomaly, the new PSOE president, Felipe Gonzalez, had committed his party to holding a referendum on the question of Spain's NATO membership. Now in government, he was under pressure to take up a position on the question himself. He soon became a convert to the idea that Spain's membership in the Alliance had not adversely affected its freedom of movement, and, far from diminishing its influence in foreign affairs, seemed to have raised its profile in Western Europe. The problem was to convince his own party of the wisdom of his conversion, and the difficulties in doing this explain why the promised referendum was delayed until 1986. The eventual policy of the PSOE was a balancing act that required consummate skills to perform: NATO membership would be supported on the French model, that is to say with no integration into military planning, and with no nuclear weapons on Spanish territory (a precedent for which already existed in the cases of Norway and Denmark). The whole NATO issue touched the roots of party politics in Spain: it was a reminder of Franco's cosy relationship with the Americans and thus many in the PSOE were instinctively antipathetic to the idea of NATO membership. Moreover, their party was sympathetic to groups, like the PLO in the Middle East and the Sandinistas in Nicaragua, with whom the United States had strong ideological differences. The right wing Alianza Popular wanted full membership of NATO; the Communists (PCE) wanted nothing to do with NATO at all, believing that Spain should be strictly neutral in the East–West conflict; and the UCD was split (not unusually), the right-wing faction (identified with Suarez) believing that Spain's participation in NATO might encourage the USSR to support terrorist groups like GRAPO and ETA in Spain while the left-wing faction (identified with Sotelo) believed pragmatically that entry into NATO was still the best way to confirm Spain's recent entry into the EEC, a policy objective that had been broadly supported right across the political spectrum.

The referendum on NATO was held on 12 March 1986. To achieve a positive result, Gonzalez knew that he was not only doing a personal U-turn but was also going against the ideological grain of his own party. One of the most powerful arguments he was able to deploy was that NATO membership would logically entail a renegotiation and reduction of the United States military presence in Spain. He also had to promise that there would be no nuclear weapons on Spanish soil, and no integration into the Alliance's military planning structure. The actual result probably mattered less for Spain than it did for the political credibility of the president. If Spain had voted 'no', little would have changed; the 'yes' vote did not solve the problem of the American bases. *The Economist* suggested, a week before the referendum, that Spain could do much less for NATO than NATO could do for Spain and concluded that if the result of the vote was against membership it would be a 'victory for the forces of the old Spain: for the narrow nationalist right that for decades preferred to huddle away from democratic Europe in behind-the-Pyrenees dictatorial isolation' (*The Economist*, 1 March 1986).

Gonzalez' victory in the referendum was due partly to his own persuasive skills, partly to the loyalty of his party, and partly to the heterogeneous nature of the anti-NATO pressure groups. A massive turnaround of public opinion would be necessary if the desired result was to be achieved, not least among his own party supporters. In a poll taken in 1984, 59 per cent of PSOE voters said they were against membership of NATO with only 13 per cent in favour (*El Pais*, 28 October 1984). In the run-up to the referendum the polls showed a minority, albeit an expanding minority, in favour of NATO membership. On 9 February 1986, 21 per cent of all those polled said they favoured NATO membership, with 38 per cent against, the remainder saying they would abstain or did not know. A week before the referendum, 26 per cent were in favour, 36 per cent against with the balance still either abstaining or saying they did not know. The eventual result was 32 per cent in favour, 24 per cent against, 4 per cent spoiled ballots, and 40 per cent abstaining (Vilanova 1987). Of those who voted, 52 per cent voted 'yes', 39 per cent voted 'no', with the remaining votes either spoiled or left blank. The lowest 'yes' vote was in the Basque country (31 per cent), and only in Navarre, Catalonia, and the Canaries, was the 'yes' vote also less than 50 per cent. During the referendum campaign Gonzalez cleverly projected an image of uncertainty if the 'yes' vote did not materialize: a general election was due that year and by linking the NATO vote to the position of his own administration, he almost succeeded in portraying the referendum as a vote of confidence in the government. The entry of Spain into the EEC only three months earlier, made it possible to argue that a withdrawal from NATO would be taken as a sign of Spanish lack of enthusiasm for European co-operation. Speaking of his conversion to NATO membership, Gonzalez rejected the view that Spain's influence had been reduced in the Alliance: 'We found that Spain's independence wasn't curtailed but strengthened, that the country's credibility was not diminished but increased. The country's views are now widely sought' (*Cambio 16*, 10 March 1986).

When the vote finally came, Gonzalez was undoubtedly helped by the fact that many in his own party voted for him, more out of loyalty than conviction, and many also abstained rather than torpedo their own government. Opposition to NATO membership came from a collection of groups on the left, and on the extreme right; the latter fearful for the effects of NATO on Spanish national sovereignty, the former basing their opposition on familiar anti-nuclear and anti-American sentiments that are well-grounded in Spanish society. The Alianza Popular (always strongly in favour of membership) had called on its supporters to abstain on the grounds that the government was opting for 'second-class membership', i.e. without full integration into the military planning structure. This ploy bred a certain amount of cynicism even inside the ranks of the Alianza but the high level of abstention in the referendum must be largely attributable to the party's tactics. At the end of the day, the opposition to NATO membership looked disunited; and the success of the Government's campaign, making heavy use of television, must be due to the fact that the issue had become one of government versus opposition, and parties versus lobby groups. Many must have asked themselves what would have happened if the 'no' vote had succeeded: there might well have been a change of government and the problem of the American bases would still need to be solved, without the intercession of NATO allies from whom, Gonzalez had argued, some support could be expected in negotiations with the United States over reducing manpower levels. Spain's role in NATO is a restricted one. It is not inevitable that Spanish troops will serve in West Germany, for example, and even Spanish naval participation in NATO exercises has been circumscribed by Anglo-Spanish friction over the Gibraltar issue, although in the summer of 1987 it was announced that, for the first time, Spanish and British ships would be part of NATO manoeuvres in the Atlantic.

Winning the referendum on NATO membership left Gonzalez with the tricky problem of how to honour the pledge, made to the electorate in the run-up to the referendum, that he would negotiate 'a substantial reduction' in the American military presence as the quid pro quo for continued NATO membership. This pledge took on a concrete form when Gonzalez requested the United States to withdraw its seventy-two F-16 fighters from the Torrejon airbase. Having seen Gonzalez do a volte-face on the question of NATO membership, the Reagan administration guessed that he might also mellow on the question of the American military presence. This was to misunderstand the political risk that Gonzalez had already taken on the NATO issue. The apparent intransigence of the Americans, and the assumed danger of having such an airbase so near Madrid, tended to galvanize Spanish opinion during 1987 behind Gonzalez. In other NATO countries, however, there has been little overt support for the stand taken by the Spanish government; and few seem to disagree with the American view that the F-16s are a vital link in the defence of the Alliance's southern flank. The aircraft have an operational area that extends as far east as Turkey and could include the Soviet Union in time of war. Spain's argument that its own recently acquired F-18s could fill the gap has not been accepted by its NATO allies. The Americans took a firm line in the negotiations with Spain not so much because of the intrinsic merits of their case, but more from a fear of creating a precedent that other West European countries might follow. The eventual outcome was a new agreement involving a reduced American presence. Spain cannot afford to throw the baby out with the bath-water: the country received $616 million from the United States in 1986. Internally, however, Gonzalez had been under pressure not to compromise: opinion polls continued to reveal strong anti-Americanism and there is still substantial support for a complete withdrawal of the whole American presence. The mayor of Torrejon was quoted as saying (in the summer of 1987) that nothing would please him more than if the Americans ploughed up their golf course and the whole air base and 'left tomorrow'. Since 1953, the mayor claimed, the Americans had done only one thing for his town: built it a go-kart track but 'they did not even give us the go-karts'. Out of the town's 100,000 inhabitants only 650 had jobs in the airbase – mainly as cleaners.

Irrespective of how integrated they are into the overall structure of NATO defences, Spain's armed forces are a substantial contribution to western defence. Spain has about 340,000 personnel in its forces of whom two-thirds are conscripts. The army has over a quarter of a million men, backed up by 500 mechanized infantry fighting-vehicles, and around 800 armoured personnel-carriers. There are various types of anti-tank weaponry including Milan, Cobra and Dragon. The Navy is the second largest in European NATO (after Britain's) with eleven destroyers, sixteen frigates and eight submarines, as well as an aircraft carrier equipped with Harrier 'jump' jets and Sea King helicopters. The Spanish Air Force employs 38,000 men and has nearly 200 aircraft, most of them Mirage jets. Spain's air defence system is its most valuable defence asset and potentially its most useful contribution to NATO's 'shield'. Code-named 'Combat Grande' it was designed by the Hughes Company in the United States who also built the NADGE system on which the rest of European NATO depends. There is therefore a high degree of compatibility between the two systems. Combat Grande consists of a series of long-range radars situated throughout Spain and linked to a central and highly sophisticated computer at the Torrejon airbase near Madrid. The central computer stores up-to-date details of all interceptor aircraft, missiles and weather conditions throughout Spain. Within 30 seconds of an enemy aircraft appearing on a radar screen the central computer will have been able to respond with an appropriate interception (Menaul 1981: 17–20).

The main thrust of Spain's NATO membership in future will lie partly in its location as a staging post between the United States and Central Europe in time of war or East–West tension, and partly in its role as defender and watchdog in the Mediterranean. The Straits of Gibraltar, linking the Atlantic and the Mediterranean, are clearly a key strategic waterway for NATO; and it is in the Alliance's task of protecting free passage, as well as monitoring Soviet ship movements, that Spain sees itself playing a part. Such a role, however, brings into focus the strategic importance of Gibraltar, and that in turn raises a crucial issue in Anglo-Spanish relations.

The Spanish claim to the British colony of Gibraltar, a promontory of only 2.25 square miles jutting out from the Andalucían coast into the Mediterranean, remains the main issue of contention between Spain and Britain, and one of the last unachieved objectives in Spanish foreign policy. The case of Gibraltar is not unique. Similar 'enclaves', remnants of vast European empires, are found in various parts of the world. They are often the object of claims by neighbouring states who press their case with varying degrees of tenacity against the metropolitan power which, more often than not, is so distant that it is forced to expend disproportionate resources to defend its possession. Sometimes the claim is backed by force and the European power loses its toehold, as Portugal did in the case of Goa in 1961; and as Britain nearly did in the case of the Falklands in 1982. More usually, however, the dispute is the subject of negotiations and diplomacy, sometimes in the United Nations, sometimes on a bilateral basis, with the aim of convincing the colonial power that the transfer of sovereignty would be reasonable, that it would be in the interests of the enclave's inhabitants, and would not in the long run be detrimental to the erstwhile colonizer. The United States faced these sorts of arguments with regard to Guantánamo (in Cuba), Spain with regard to Ceuta and Melilla (its two enclaves in North Africa) and Britain with regard to Gibraltar. The pursuit of these claims through diplomatic channels does not exclude, on occasions, various forms of bravado, blockades and boycotts. Spain's characterization of Gibraltar as the 'last colony in Europe' and the circumstances in which the territory was wrested from her, combine to make the issue a potent thorn in the flesh of Spain's national *amour propre*.

Gibraltar became *de facto* a British possession in 1704 when it was seized by Admiral Rooke during the War of Spanish Succession, and Britain's legal title to the Rock was enshrined in the Treaty of Utrecht (1713). In the Treaty of Versailles (1783) at the end of the War of American Independence, Spain retained Minorca and received Florida in exchange for a cessation of hostilities against Gibraltar. In the period since 1945, Gibraltar has been discussed at the United Nations. In 1960 it was listed, along with other territories, in a resolution of the General Assembly calling for their decolonization. In 1965, a UN committee on decolonization urged diplomatic negotiations between Spain and Britain over Gibraltar and, two years later, in an attempt to ascertain the wishes of the Gibraltarians themselves, a plebiscite was held in the colony which showed an overwhelming majority in favour of remaining under British rule (12,138 votes to 44). In 1969, the Spanish government exerted extra pressure by effectively sealing the frontier between Gibraltar and the border town of La Línea. No pedestrian or motor-traffic was allowed to cross; no goods could cross in either direction; and telephone links were severed. Although telephone links were restored in 1977, after the transition to democratic government in Spain, the blockade remained in place until the early 1980s. The effects of the blockade were to alienate Gibraltarian opinion further from the country that claimed it, to make Gibraltar more dependent on Britain (and on Moroccans who replaced the 5,000 workers who had formerly crossed the frontier daily to make a living in, amongst other things, Gibraltar's important dockyard), and to impoverish the town of La Línea and its hinterland for which Gibraltar had been an important source of jobs, trade and income. Elections in Gibraltar in February 1980 produced an overwhelming mandate for parties opposed to any weakening of the link with Britain: the only party campaigning for Gibraltarian autonomy failed to win a seat in the 15-seat legislature. There was '... no sign that the rebirth of democracy in Spain [had] led the Gibraltarians to lend a more favourable ear to its claims' (*The Economist*, 16 February 1980).

The Lisbon agreement (1980) was the first step in a new relationship between Spain and Britain over Gibraltar, although the effects of the agreement were slow to materialize, due partly to animosities aroused during the Falklands war, and partly to misunderstandings arising from the agreement itself. In the Spanish media, the view was taken that the British government was placing too much emphasis on the opening of the frontier as if it were primarily a bargaining counter to facilitate Spain's entry into the EEC, and a measure to boost Andalucía's failing economy, whereas the Spanish saw the Lisbon Agreement as a mutually beneficial attempt to remove an obstacle between the two countries. As the wording of the agreement put it, the governments had agreed to 'resolve the Gibraltar problem in a spirit of friendship and in accordance with the appropriate United Nations resolutions. The two governments have agreed to open negotiations with a view to settling all their differences over Gibraltar' (*The Economist*, 19 April 1980). On several occasions, the Spanish authorities postponed the reopening of the frontier until they finally relented, and then only for pedestrians, in 1982. In the two years since the Lisbon Agreement, the only concessions had been extremely modest: Spanish language programmes were broadcast in Gibraltar, and in turn the Spanish allowed butane-gas imports into Gibraltar.

If the decision of Prince Charles and his new wife to spend the first night of their honeymoon in Gibraltar played some part in further irritating Anglo-Spanish relations in the summer of 1981, it was nothing to the sensitivities provoked by the Falklands War the following year. It was not only that Spanish public opinion, in contrast to most of Western Europe, was solidly behind the Argentinian claim to the Falklands, but salt was rubbed into wounds when Gibraltar's dockyard and repair facilities became a key port of call for ships involved in the Falklands War. The British view was that there could be no meaningful negotiations until Spain opened the frontier; the Spanish view seems to have been that steps towards decolonizing Gibraltar should precede (or at least accompany) any relaxation of border restrictions.

It was in this atmosphere of impasse that the new Socialist government came to power in 1982. On the one hand the Gonzalez administration clearly understood that the frontier blockade was serving only to alienate Gibraltar, and was a real hindrance to the economic development of Andalucía (an area where the PSOE had substantial support); but on the other hand, the new government was anxious to assert its patriotic credentials in a country that had not seen Socialists in power for half a century, and where only a couple of years previously the whole constitutional form of government had nearly collapsed in a military coup. The Gibraltar issue provided the virility test of patriotism in foreign policy. In moving to unfreeze the blockage between the two countries, the government needed to extract reciprocal concessions from Britain, if only to demonstrate to its political opponents that it was not prepared to kowtow on an issue of national pride.

In February 1985, the frontier was finally opened between Gibraltar and Spain. In achieving this agreement the Spanish and British foreign ministers both emphasized that the interests of the Gibraltarians themselves should remain paramount. A matter of principle remains as an obstacle between the two countries reaching a final solution. The Spanish insist that the matter of 'sovereignty' must be included in any meaningful negotiations, while the British, mindful of the 1967 plebiscite, insist that 'sovereignty' is the one topic which is not negotiable. The people of Gibraltar have undoubtedly benefited from the opening of the border, as has the immediate hinterland in Spain. However, better economic conditions in Gibraltar seem likely to delay rather than hasten any solution involving a political *rapprochement* between Gibraltar and Spain. The Gibraltarian economy remains heavily dependent on Britain. Two-thirds of Gibraltar's imports come from Britain; Britain is the source of two-thirds of Gibraltar's income; and the British Ministry of Defence pays two-thirds of the salaries in Gibraltar. Twenty-three per cent of the jobs in Gibraltar are related directly to shipbuilding and repairs; 22 per cent are in construction; and 14 per cent in retail trades. The British plan to privatize the dockyard gradually has raised fears in the colony that Britain's will to support the local economy may not be limitless: the speed with which the British government negotiated the return of Hong Kong to China (albeit under different circumstances) sent shivers down the spines of Gibraltar's politicians.

Spain's membership of NATO and the EEC alters the context in which a solution to the problem of Gibraltar may be found. However, the possibilities are probably not as extensive as the Spanish government likes to think. Until recently, Spain used the British presence in Gibraltar as a pretext for not participating in joint naval exercises with other NATO countries. The Spanish suggestion of some kind of joint control of the port in Gibraltar, under NATO auspices, is attractive at first sight until one remembers that nuclear weapons are banned from Spanish harbours (would they insist on this in Gibraltar too?) and that Spain is not in NATO's military planning group. How effective would joint supervision of the Straits be in that case?

The Spanish policy towards the Gibraltar issue can be summed up as follows. The claim over Gibraltar is a cardinal feature of Spanish foreign policy. The claim is supported by the economic and personal links that exist between the Rock and the Spanish hinterland. The presence of Spain in NATO makes it incomprehensible that Britain should assume the role of the Alliance's sole representative in Gibraltar when Spain's security is more obviously at stake in the region. The extension of EEC rights to people living in Gibraltar and in Spain on an equal basis, and the freeing of trade throughout the EEC, make the border between the Rock and the Spanish mainland something of an anachronism. The United Nations has made several pronouncements that Spain regards as favourable to her, and place the onus on Britain to make the running in finding a solution. The Treaty of Utrecht stipulates that Gibraltar should revert to Spain if Britain should for any reason decide to relinquish it. The Spanish government concedes, however, that to take the Rock by force would be senseless, and that any solution should take into account the interests of Gibraltar's inhabitants. From Spain's point of view there are five essential elements to any mutually satisfactory solution to the Gibraltar problem: first, it has to be recognized that Gibraltar is a part of Spain currently occupied by Britain; second, that decolonization has been sanctioned by the United Nations and should therefore be acted upon by Britain; third, that bilateral negotiations are the only way to restore Gibraltar to Spain; fourth, that the local population must have its interests respected in the re-integration of Gibraltar into Spain, but that this does not mean that the people of Gibraltar have a right to self-determination; and, fifth, that the Spanish Constitution provides unprecedented scope for Gibraltar to retain a degree of autonomy under the Spanish Crown compatible with both the interests of its people and those of Spain as a whole (Shub and Carr 1985: 110). In the absence of any political solution in the foreseeable future, the economic ties and functional co-operation in the Gibraltar region continue. Pollution control measures in the Bay of Algeciras are the subject of joint Spanish–Gibraltarian negotiations; but the limits to co-operation are still evident in the fears aroused in Gibraltar itself by a recent proposal that passengers landing at Gibraltar airport should be allowed to proceed directly to the Costa del Sol without passing through British immigration controls. This chipping away at British sovereignty was seen as the thin end of a wedge by Gibraltar's politicians. On their part, the Spanish displayed a similar sensitivity (although on economic rather than political grounds) when in 1987 they vetoed the inclusion of Gibraltar in an EEC plan for deregulated airfares in Western Europe.

Spain and the EEC

When Spain and Portugal joined the EEC on 1 January 1986, they brought the total number of members to twelve, and the population of the Community to 320 million. It was the third enlargement of the EEC: in 1973 the original Six expanded northwards and became Nine as Britain, Ireland, and Denmark became members. Then in 1981 the Community looked south and accepted Greece as the tenth member state, a process that was continued with the entry of Portugal and Spain in 1986. Spain's arrival marked the culmination of seven years of negotiations, and sixteen years of preferential trade with the EEC following the signing of a limited agreement with the Six in 1970. This agreement covered about 95 per cent of EEC industrial imports from Spain subject to tariffs, and 62 per cent of agricultural imports; while about 60 per cent of Spanish imports from the Community were affected. The admission of new member states is governed by Article 237 of the Rome Treaty where it is specified that any European state can apply for membership subject to the unanimous approval of the Council of Ministers.

The length of the negotiations between Spain and the Ten reflected real conflicts of economic interest between the two sides. What pushed the negotiations forward and ensured that they would, despite the obstacles encountered en route, reach a successful conclusion, was the belief on both sides that political considerations should be paramount. In Western Europe Spain's membership of the European Economic Community was perceived as the surest way of anchoring Spain's nascent democracy in the bedrock of viable political institutions.

The negotiations began in February 1979, nearly two years after the formal application had been lodged by Spain with the Council of Ministers. The delay in getting things under way was due to understandable caution on the part of some EEC governments. Agriculture, for example, had long been seen as an area of contention given the importance of farming in the Spanish economy (6 per cent of GDP compared with 3.5 per cent on average in the Community), and the 30 per cent extra land under cultivation that Spain would bring to the EEC. Nor was Spanish agriculture complementary to the needs of the Ten: on the one hand there was huge capacity in products like citrus fruits, olive oil and wine while in other respects such as cereals, milk and meat, Spain's productivity lagged behind the Community. Fishing proved to be one of the toughest items on the agenda, and was one of the last issues to be settled. The sheer size of Spain's fishing fleet, its tonnage equal to half that of the Ten's combined, posed a threat to the livelihood of fishermen in other parts of the EEC unless special provisions were made to protect them. Industrially, Spain was bringing a mixed dowry to the wedding feast: her shipbuilding industry was one of the largest in the world; and she had become the biggest exporter of cars in Western Europe. Nevertheless, many of her industries were less competitive than those of her rivals and it would only be after painful restructuring that the opportunities of an extended 'home' market of 320 million consumers could be realized. In the meantime, Spain's negotiators would seek to prolong the traditional period for removing protective tariffs for as long as possible.

Despite obvious areas of difficulty, the EEC could not have postponed serious negotiations for ever if the Community's reputation as a grouping open to all European democracies was to remain credible. France was the most reluctant negotiator throughout due to justified fears that agriculture· and, especially viticulture, in the south-west of the country would be ruined by Spanish competition. In 1978, 1979 and 1981, there were elections in France and these effectively stalled any concessions that the French might make to smooth the path of negotiation.

In June 1980, the Spanish government announced that it was going to apply for NATO membership based on a simple majority vote in the Cortes. The purpose of this rather ill-considered move was to break the deadlock in the EEC negotiations by offering something thought to be highly desirable to Spain's EEC partners-to-be. The ploy failed partly because France, the main obstacle in the negotiations, was not a full member of NATO and not much impressed therefore by Spain's sudden enthusiasm to join, and partly because it was apparent to most observers that NATO membership, not being based on a broad consensus in Spain, was likely to prove problematic in future should there be a change of government. Spain added a rider to its NATO application to the effect that progress must be made on the Gibraltar question, a condition that looked reasonable in the wake of the Lisbon Agreement signed earlier in the year.

In March 1982, Spain dropped its long-standing resistance to the introduction of VAT, a stance that had provided the French with a reliable pretext for treading water on other aspects of the negotiations. The French now argued, instead, that 'reform' of the EEC's budgetary mechanisms must precede Spanish entry since the arrival of two additional agricultural countries in the Community would pose insuperable burdens on its finances.

The victory of a Socialist government in Spain in 1982 heralded a long period of agonizing over NATO membership that was only resolved after a referendum in 1986 in which the ruling PSOE advised its followers to reverse the party's traditionally anti-NATO stance. In the meantime, in early 1984, while it held the presidency of the Council of Ministers, the French government dangled the 'carrot' of Spain being allowed into the EEC as a quid pro quo for French demands on budgetary reform being accepted. Although the bait was not taken when offered, the Community did manage, in the next twelve months, to achieve progress on the financial issue and, at the same time, resolve the outstanding problems regarding Spanish entry. The Treaty of Accession was signed in Madrid on 12 June 1985.

The main features of the treaty can be usefully summarized at this point. Spain was allocated two commissioners in the 17-man commission (Mañuel Marin and Abel Matutes from the PSOE and AP parties respectively) and 60 seats in the European Parliament (now with 518 seats). In the enlarged Parliament, meeting for the first time on 13 January 1986, the Spanish delegation was made up of appointees from the Cortes pending the direct election of MEPs in 1987. Spain has the usual representation in the Court of Justice in Luxembourg, and on the Economic and Social Council (an advisory body). Customs duties are being dismantled over seven years and in eight stages. Quotas are abolished on imports except in a few cases where Spain feels the need for protection in the short term, e.g. colour television sets. For three years Spanish steel exports will be subject to quantitative limits and during the same period the Spanish steel industry will be allowed to receive subsidies designed to achieve restructuring along the lines of Community steel policy. VAT was to be introduced at once in Spain, who, in turn, had to apply the whole range of policies achieved in the Community such as competition policy, transport, consumer and environment policies. Some temporary derogations have been allowed: for example, on the fitting of tachographs in certain vehicles; on the lead content of premium grade petrol; and on pharmaceutical standards.

In agriculture, customs duties will be abolished in stages while price and subsidy levels rise gradually to meet those in the rest of the Community. During the transitional period of seven years, price gaps are being offset by 'accession compensatory amounts' that work like a sluice-gate to adjust the prices of goods crossing frontiers in either direction between the old and new member states. There are additional measures to cover products that particularly concern the existing member states. Wine will be subject to a production ceiling and any surplus has to be sent for distillation. To avoid a surplus in olive oil, the transitional arrangements will last ten years, and Spanish import controls can be maintained for the first five years. For fruit and vegetables, a ten-year transitional phase also applies, and Community prices will not begin to apply until after the first four-year period has elapsed. Due to the size of the Spanish fishing fleet, there are limits to the numbers that are allowed to fish at any one time; certain zones off Ireland and Britain are closed to Spanish boats until after 1996; and the Spanish fishing fleet is expected to be restructured (i.e. its numbers reduced) in the meantime. The principle of free movement of workers in the EEC is restricted in the case of Spanish workers until 1992 (1995 in the case of Luxembourg) but Spanish workers and their families resident abroad in 1985 may remain where they are.

Spain automatically accepts on its entry to the EEC the wide range of trade agreements, their benefits and constraints, made between the EEC and the rest of the world. However, special consideration is to be given to the protection of imports from North Africa which are in danger of being replaced by the inclusion of Spain and Portugal in the customs union of the EEC. At the same time there is likely to be scope for greater trade with Latin America in the Community's pattern of overseas commercial agreements; and the presence of Spain in the EEC makes it a likely bridgehead from which such new initiatives could be launched.

During the long periods of frustrating diplomacy that preceded accession, Spanish public opinion remained remarkably supportive of the country's intended role in the EEC. The goal of Community membership has consistently commanded widespread support in all the main political parties and, as a political issue, is virtually unique in uniting the Church, the Army, the trade unions and big business in a common cause. This consensus is reflected in grass-roots opinion. Surveys of public attitudes, carried out at regular intervals by the European Commission, make it possible to chart the 'European mood' in Spain during the period leading up to EEC entry and beyond. Between 1980 and 1984, the Community's polls show that there was an increasing awareness of and interest in the EEC. Those claiming to be 'very interested' in Community affairs rose from 32 per cent to 35 per cent while those who felt Community matters to be 'very important' rose from 21 per cent to 31 per cent between 1982 and 1984 (Eurobarometer 1984). Although Spain has been a member of the European Economic Community for a relatively short time, popular support for membership seems to be as high as it is in countries with much longer time-frames from which to judge the benefits. This almost instinctive support for the EEC in Spain confirms the hypothesis that it is not the economic advantages but the political implications of membership that appeal to most Spaniards. There has been increasing support for the general notion of 'Western European unification': the proportion of those claiming to be broadly in favour rose from 65 per cent to 75 per cent between early 1985 and late 1986 (Eurobarometer 1986). When asked more specifically about Spain's membership of the EEC, 66 per cent believe it is 'a good thing', and only 4 per cent a 'bad thing' (November 1986), the remainder not committing themselves one way or the other. In Britain by way of contrast, only 42 per cent believe British membership is a 'good thing' and 27 per cent bad (Eurobarometer 1986).

However, when Spanish respondents are asked if they feel the country has benefited from membership, most are sure that it has not, although those taking this view dropped from 65 per cent to 52 per cent during the first year of membership (Eurobarometer 1986), while those feeling that the country had benefited rose from 9 per cent to 20 per cent in the same period. The contrast between Spaniards' support for their country's membership of the EEC and negative feelings about the benefits that have accrued can be explained partly by a belief that the political arguments, although less tangible, outweigh the economic ones, and partly by an optimism that the economic fruits of membership will, in any case, take longer to materialize. This latter sentiment reflects a realistic assessment of the country's ability to compete in the Community of Twelve. A painful period of restructuring and adaptation must be undergone before the full benefits of the extended market can be achieved.

Spain's position in the Community today can be compared to that of Britain in 1973; in both cases a world language and the remnants of imperial responsibilities make the European arena seem somewhat restricted, however necessary accession may be to maximize the export opportunities offered by a customs union. However, unlike Britain, which for so long held back from participation in the EEC because it felt that its political priorities lay elsewhere, Spain's entry to the Community is the culmination of a long campaign to restore democracy to the country and underwrite this by linking the potential benefits of membership to support within Spain for democratic institutions. It is not simply the negative threat of the EEC refusing to tolerate the membership of a country that abandons democratic practices, it is the subtler and more positive inducement provided by wide sectors of Spanish society identifying enthusiastically with the 'role-models' of other West European economies. The feeling in Spain that the country is 'somewhere at last' is mixed with both fear and optimism at the problems and prospects, respectively, offered by membership. The Spanish prime minister caught this mood when he called Spanish accession a *desafío* (a challenge): it will be necessary to wear the sackcloth of industrial shakeouts before putting on the brighter garments of booming trade and rising prosperity.

Spain's membership of the EEC has already begun to reshape its relationship with the Mediterranean region; and during the NATO debate it was often pointed out by anti-NATO opinion that the Central European front was a long way from Spain and of much less strategic importance than North Africa, an area not covered by the NATO Treaty. Spain's foreign policy continues to be based on the assumption that it can act as a 'bridge' between Europe and Africa and that the Mediterranean ought to become a region that excludes superpower rivalry and adopts a neutralist stance akin to the Nordic area, and with the same beneficial implications for East–West security. In contrast to her West European partners, Spain has followed a relatively benign policy towards the Arab countries of the Middle East. This is almost entirely due to Spain's dependence on the Arab countries for oil: at the end of the 1970s two-thirds of its energy needs had to be imported and its energy deficit accounted for 90 per cent of its trade deficit. The gravity of that situation is underlined when we appreciate that in 1970, Spain's energy deficit had accounted for only one-fifth of its total trade shortfall. The explosion of oil prices in 1973–4, and again at the end of the decade, dealt a serious blow to the Spanish economy at a time when it was on a wave of steady expansion. Indigenous energy reserves (oil and natural gas) are now being exploited, and it is hoped to reduce dependence upon imported oil, at least, to about 43 per cent of needs by 1990. Over half of Spain's oil imports have come traditionally from Saudi Arabia and Iran; but attempts to diversify sources of supply have involved Mexico, Venezuela, and Iraq as alternatives. Spain's failure until recently to recognize the state of Israel was linked to its support of the Arab position in the Middle East. Spain's accession to the EEC involved it in aligning itself with common foreign policy positions already adopted by the Ten. Thus, in January 1986, Spain formally recognized Israel, and it seems likely that as the EEC itself has moved nearer the position adopted by Spain on the Middle East, there should be little difficulty in achieving coherence in Community policy in the future. When it recognized Israel, the Spanish government was careful to give reassurances to the Arab countries, a sure sign that it still regards its energy needs as a crucial ingredient in foreign policy. Spain's policy on the Middle East has obviously put some distance between itself and the United States, and the negotiations between the Spanish government and the United States over the American bases are part of a broader scenario where Spain does not want its territory to be associated in any way with the American foreign policy in the Middle East.

As Britain still devotes considerable resources to maintaining political influence in its Commonwealth, so Spain looks to Latin America as a region where a common language and a colonial past provide the foundations for economic co-operation, mutual diplomatic support, trade links and cultural ties. During the Franco era, relations with Latin America were neglected in the sense that the Caudillo used the New World as a focus for grandiloquent speeches on the theme of *Hispanidad* ('Greater Spain') and he welcomed fellow dictators like Batista and Trujillo to Madrid on state occasions; but there was little practical assistance for the nascent development of the hemisphere whose political and economic fortunes were more deeply affected, for better or worse, by the United States. The attitudes of other Latin American countries towards the Franco regime were undoubtedly coloured by the fact that they became a refuge for political exiles from Spain. Today, those Latin American countries, still in the throes of dictatorship or struggling democracy, look to Spain as a model of what can be achieved in a short space of time, and with little turmoil. Intellectuals and politicians have returned to Spain and both they and the refugees from Latin American military rule keep fresh the personal and cultural links between the two continents. There has also been significant emigration from Spain in this century, as in the last, and these ties of kith and kin make Latin America as familiar to many Spaniards as Australia and New Zealand are to the British. In both cases, joining the European Economic Community involved a psychological readjustment that may take decades to complete. The importance of Latin America in Spanish foreign policy is enshrined in the Spanish Constitution where Article 56 makes the King supreme in foreign relations and 'especially in the nations which constitute its historic community'. The King has visited Latin America frequently and these ceremonial visits are now paralleled by growing trade with the region, and increasing investment in infrastructure projects. Spanish banks have a substantial presence in Latin America, second only to that of the United States. Under the Socialist government, Spain's policy towards Latin America is based on the principles of non-interference in their domestic affairs; the upholding of human rights; and participation in economic aid projects that are to the mutual advantage of both partners.

The centre-piece of PSOE policy towards Central America is the Plan de Cooperación Integral which has been administered by the Institute for Latin American Co-operation in conjunction with the Ministry of Employment. The Plan started in 1984 with a budget of 200 million pesetas, a sum that had been quadrupled by 1987. The principal foci of the Plan were Nicaragua, Honduras and Costa Rica, the latter being the largest recipient of aid in the region. The aid programmes are based on joint ventures between Spain and the host country. The aid is still on a small scale with an emphasis on light industry, communications, and the modernization of agricultural techniques. The purpose of the aid is to express a commitment to the long-term eradication of economic and social deprivation of which the current violence is seen as a short-term symptom. In wishing to see the restoration of stable democracy in Central America, Spain is well aware that the external environment is a contributor to the region's problems; until the imbalances in trade between the richer and poorer countries are resolved, and until the east–west conflict no longer makes the region its plaything, it is unlikely that the governments of the area will be able to stand on their own two feet and feel free of both political and economic exploitation. Spain has therefore strong reservations about United States policy in Central America, even if the objections are now voiced in a more muted way. On the other hand, Spain does not support Soviet influence in the Caribbean, nor have relations between the PSOE and the Sandinistas been all that warm recently. Spain does not wish, and is not able, to play the part of mediator in the region's conflict, but it does feel that its broader role in defusing East–West tensions in other parts of the world (especially Western Europe) could play a part in freeing the Caribbean area from the side-effects of that superpower competition to which it is vulnerable (Grugel 1987).

Spain's role in Latin America generally is pulled two ways by virtue of its membership of both NATO and the EEC: the latter organization being far from happy with the United States policy towards Nicaragua. Many Latin American countries, struggling to work out their own forms of democracy free from interference by either superpower, appreciate the advocacy of their cause in Spain within the European Economic Community. More broadly, Latin America feels that the Community has neglected them and looks to Spain to argue their case in the future. So far, however, there has been little evidence to show that the Community has been greatly affected by Spanish interest in the New World. It also has to be said that there are limits to what Spain itself can achieve in Latin America. Its economy is classified by the OECD in the same category as Brazil and South Korea (as a 'newly-industrialized country') and many of Spain's own industries in fact duplicate, rather than complement, those of the Third World: textiles, steel, shipbuilding and car assembly.

In sum, there are a number of contradictions and ambiguities in Spanish foreign policy. Although a member of NATO, Spain is still an opponent of many aspects of American foreign policy; although a member of the EEC, Spain is equally concerned with North Africa, and feels that it cannot totally ignore Latin America; although it has deep sympathies with both the underdeveloped world and the non-aligned nations, it cannot throw its lot in with them completely; although in the Middle East it now recognizes Israel, it must still court the goodwill of Arab nations; and although it pursues its irredentist claim to Gibraltar, it must resist apparently analogous Moroccan claims to the enclaves of Melilla and Ceuta. Within the European Economic Community, Spain is expected to consult her partners in matters of foreign policy via the mechanisms of European

Political Co-operation (EPC). A study of Spanish voting at the United Nations in 1979 and 1980 showed a growing convergence between itself and the EEC countries over Middle East matters but less so on disarmament questions and topics related to Africa (Shub and Carr 1985). In the future, the habits of co-operation pursued in the EPC will mark out the parameters within which foreign policy decisions can be taken, thereby achieving a greater consistency.

Bibliography

Abel, C. and Torrents, N. (1984) *Spain: Conditional Democracy*, Beckenham: Croom Helm

Almond, G. and Verba, S. (1963) *The Civic Culture*, Boston: Little & Brown

Amnesty International, (1987) *Annual Report*

Arbos, X. (1985) 'Central vs peripheral nationalisms in building democracy: the case of Spain', Barcelona: ECPR Workshops

Ball, A. (1983) *Modern Politics and Government*, London: Macmillan

Bell, D. (ed.) (1983) *Democratic Politics in Spain*, London: Pinter

Bonime-Blanc, A. (1987) *Spain's Transition to Democracy: the politics of constitution making*, Boulder, Colo.: Westview

Brewer, J., Guelke, A., Hume, I., Moxon-Browne, E. and Wilford, R. (1988) *The Police, Public Order and the State*, London: Macmillan

Burton, F. (1978) *The Politics of Legitimacy*, London: Routledge & Kegan Paul

Caciagli, M. (1984) 'Spain: parties and the party system in transition', *West European Politics*, 7, 2, 84–97

Carr, R. (1980) *Modern Spain 1875–1980*, Oxford: Oxford University Press

Carr, R. and Fusi, J. P. (1979) *Spain: from dictatorship to democracy*, London: Allen & Unwin

Conradt, D. (1986) *The German Polity*, London: Longman

Dahlerup, D. (1986) *The New Women's Movement*, London: Sage

Diaz Lopez, C. (1982) 'The politicization of Galician cleavages', in S. Rokkan and D. Urwin (eds) *The Politics of Territorial Identity*, London: Sage

Donaghy, P. and Newton, M. (1987) *Spain: a guide to political and economic institutions*, Cambridge: Cambridge University Press

Eurobarometer, (1984, 1985, 1986, 1987) Brussels: EEC Commission

Fogarty, M., Ryan, I. and Lee, J. (1984) *Irish Values and Attitudes*, Dublin: Dominican Publications

Garmendia, J. (1980) *Historia de ETA*, San Sebastian: Itxaropena

Gilmour, D. (1986) *The Transformation of Spain*, London: Quartet Books

Gispert, C. and Prats, J. (1978) *España: un estado plurinacional*, Barcelona: Editorial Blume

Graham, R. (1984) *Spain: change of a nation*, London: Michael Joseph

Grugel, J. (1987) 'Spain's Socialist government and Central American dilemmas', *International Affairs*, 63, 4

Gunther, R. (1985) 'Un análisis preliminar de las alteraciónes producidas en 1982 en el sistema español de partidos', *Revista de Estudios Politicos*, 45, 7 *et seq.*

Gunther, R., Sani, G. and Shabad, G. (1986) *Spain after Franco*, Berkeley, Calif.: University of California Press

Harding, S. (1986) *Contrasting Values in Western Europe*, London: Macmillan

Hechter, M. (1974) *Internal Colonialism*, London: Allen & Unwin

Heskin, K. (1980) *Northern Ireland: a psychological analysis*, Dublin: Gill and Macmillan

Heywood, P. (1987) 'Spain: 10 June 1987', *Government and Opposition*, 22, 4, 390–401

Hooper, J. (1987) *The Spaniards: a portrait of the new Spain*, Harmondsworth: Penguin

Hudson, R. and Lewis, J. (1985) *Uneven Development in Southern Europe*, London: Methuen

Inglehart-Reilly, M. (1986) 'The political mobilization of Spanish women compared to other women of Western Europe', *American Political Science Association*

Lancaster, T. (1987) 'Comparative nationalism: the Basques in Spain and France', *European Journal of Political Research*, 15, 5, 561–90

Lancaster, T. and Prevost, G. (1985) *Politics and Change in Spain*, New York: Praeger

Linz, J. (1980) 'The new Spanish party system', in R. Rose (ed.) *Electoral Participation: a comparative analysis*, London: Sage, pp. 102–10

Lodge, J. (1988) *The Threat of Terrorism*, Brighton: Wheatsheaf

Lopez-Pintor, R. (1982) *La opinión pública española: del franquismo a la democracia*, Madrid: Centro de Investigaciónes Sociologicas

Lovenduski, J. (1986) *Women and European Politics*, Brighton: Wheatsheaf

MacMillion, C. (1981) 'International integration and international disintegration', *Comparative Politics*, 13, 33, 291–312

Maravall, J. (1982) *The Transition to Democracy in Spain*, Beckenham: Croom Helm

Marcus, J. (1983) 'The triumph of Spanish Socialism: the 1982 Election', *West European Politics*, 6, 3 281–6

Mayo, P. E. (1974) *The Roots of Identity*, London: Allen Lane

Medhurst, K. (1982) *The Basques and Catalans*, London: Minority Rights Group

Melich, A., Viros, R. and Treserra, M. (1985) 'Some remarks on national identity: an example about Catalonia', Barcelona: ECPR Workshops

Menaul, S. (1981) 'The geo-strategic importance of the Iberian Peninsula', *Conflict Studies*, 133, Institute for the Study of Conflict

Merkl, P., (1986) *Political Violence and Terror*, Berkeley, Calif.: University of California Press

Moxon-Browne, E. (1983) 'Spain at the threshold of the European Community', *Contemporary Review*, 243

Moxon-Browne, E. (1987) *Spain and the ETA: the bid for Basque autonomy*, London: Centre for Security and Conflict Studies

Norris, P. (1987) *Politics and Sexual Equality*, Brighton: Wheatsheaf

Northedge, F. (1974) *The Foreign Policies of the Powers*, London: Faber

Orizo, F. (1983) *España entre la Apatía y el Cambio Social*, Madrid: Editorial Mapfre

Penniman, H. and Mujal Leon, E. (1985) *Spain at the polls, 1977, 1979, and 1982*, Durham, NC: Duke University Press

Pollack, B. (1987) *The Paradox of Spanish Foreign Policy*, London: Pinter

Pollack, B. and Hunter, G. (1987) 'Spanish democracy after four elections', *Parliamentary Affairs*, **40**

Preston, P. (ed.) (1986) *The Triumph of Democracy in Spain*, London: Methuen

Prevost, G. (1984) 'Change and continuity in the Spanish labour movement', *West European Politics*, 7, 4, 80–94

Reynolds, P. (1980) *An Introduction to International Relations*, London: Longman

Roach, J. and Thomaneck, J. (1985) *Police and Public Order in Europe*, Beckenham: Croom Helm

Robinson, R. (1987) 'From change to continuity: the 1986 Spanish Election', *West European Politics*, 10, 120–4

Rokkan, S. and Urwin, D. (eds) (1982) *The Politics of Territorial Identity*, London: Sage

Rose, R. (ed.) (1980) *Electoral Participation: a comparative analysis*, London: Sage

Sartori, G. (1978) *Parties and Party Systems: a framework for analysis*, Cambridge: Cambridge University Press

Schumpeter, J. (1961) *Capitalism, Socialism and Democracy*, Oxford: Oxford University Press

Seligson, M. and Muller, E. (1987) 'Democratic stability and economic crisis: Costa Rica 1978–83', *International Studies Quarterly*, 31, 301–26

Share, D. (1985) 'Two transitions: democratization and the evolution of the Spanish Left, *West European Politics*, **8**, 1

Shub, J. and Carr, R. (1985) *Spain: studies in political security*, New York: Praeger

Sullivan, J. (1988) *ETA and Basque Nationalism*, London: Routledge

Tamames, R. (1986) *The Spanish Economy*, London: Hurst

Threlfall, M. (1985) 'The Women's Movement in Spain', *New Left Review*, **151**, 44–73.

Treverton, G. (1986) *Spain: domestic politics and security policy*, London: International Institute for Strategic Studies

Valles, J. and Foix, M. (1988) 'Decentralization in Spain: a review', *European Journal of Political Research*, **16**

Vilanova, P. (1987) 'Le mode de participation du mouvement anti-OTAN: le cas de l'Espagne', Barcelona: ECPR Workshops

Williams, C. (1982) *National Separatism*, Cardiff: University of Wales Press

Women of Europe (1986, 1987) Brussels: EEC Commission

Index

For Product Safety Concerns and Information please contact our EU
representative GPSR@taylorandfrancis.com
Taylor & Francis Verlag GmbH, Kaufingerstraße 24, 80331 München, Germany